The Laureate's Choice Anthology

The Laureate's Choice Anthology

smith|doorstop

Published 2019 by
Smith|Doorstop books
The Poetry Business
Campo House
54 Campo Lane
Sheffield S1 2EG
www.poetrybusiness.co.uk

ISBN 978-1-912196-76-0

British Library Cataloguing-in-Publication Data.
A catalogue record for this book is available from the
British Library.

Cover design by Utter
Inner by Tim Morris
Printed and bound by CPI Group (UK) Ltd, Croydon, CR0 4YY

Smith|Doorstop is a member of Inpress,
www.inpressbooks.co.uk. Distributed by NBN International, Airport Business
Centre, 10 Thornbury Road Plymouth PL 6 7PP.

The Poetry Business receives financial support from
Arts Council England

Supported by
ARTS COUNCIL
ENGLAND

CONTENTS

Tom Sastry

Karen Smith

ZEINA HASHEM BECK

Zeina Hashem Beck is a Lebanese poet. Her first collection, *To Live in Autumn*, won the 2013 Backwaters Prize. Her second collection, *Louder than Hearts*, won the 2016 May Sarton NH Poetry Prize. She's also the author of *3arabi Song*, winner of the 2016 Rattle Chapbook Prize. She's been nominated for the Pushcart Prize, Best of the Net, and the Forward Prize. Her work has appeared in *Ploughshares*, *Poetry*, and *The Rialto*, among others, and her poem 'Maqam' won the 2017 Frederick Bock Prize from *Poetry* Magazine. *There Was and How Much There Was* was published as a Laureate's Choice in 2016.

When I was a little girl I hated afternoons. I didn't know what to do with them – they made me feel empty and bored. I repeatedly complained to my mother, "I want to CREATE things! How do we CREATE things?" Perhaps this question already carried in it the urge to write, even before I had learnt how. I grew up in a house where there weren't many books. I didn't do much reading as a child, but I was still surrounded by stories: the street outside, the carpenter downstairs, the butcher who hung a cow from a hook, the school next door, the archbishopric next to that, and the women – my mother, my aunts, Mom's friends, the neighbours.

There Was and How Much There Was is a literal translation of the Arabic 'kan ya ma kan', usually translated as 'once upon a time.' I love the literal translation because of the abundance it suggests. The women in this chapbook, be they real or imaginary, have an abundance of stories, of joy and grief, of anger and love. They are Arab women, but they're also simply women: tired of the men who want to define them – lovers, brothers, husbands, sons, God. It makes a difference how we define and redefine ourselves and the world around us.

Last week I spoke angrily to my husband about how civil marriage should be implemented in Lebanon, to give women more power and to facilitate interfaith marriages like ours. Somewhere in our conversation my husband said, "Zeina, you can't change years and years of patriarchy." He meant not immediately, and yes, I'm aware of that. But I can't sit through the long empty afternoons. I have to try to CREATE a space, no matter how small, for creating, telling stories, slowing down, asking questions, reaching out.

Recipes

The night before I left, you wrote me recipes,
said, *God help us, you don't even know*
how to cook rice, then smiled and added,
Good for you. All night you wrote
about lentils, eggplants, yogurt, peas,
included notes like, *Don't daydream,*
remember the fire / Watch out
for the steam as you lift the lid /
Don't burn your eyelashes when you look
into the oven. An airplane and a few weeks
later, I went through your notes and found
a little prayer. *I hope,*
it read, *I hope you'll forgive*
the mistakes I've made. I knew

what you meant – those afternoons
you pulled at your hair, lay crying
on the bed, told me, *Even Allah*
can't stand you right now. How you chased me
around the house, waved your slipper, flung it
like a boomerang. That time you slapped me
across the face, then walked barefoot
down the building stairs. The days you said,
I don't want to hear you say the word
mama anymore. Ever.

So I called you, said things like
Hi like *The weather* like *My hips*
are getting wider by the second.
I told you I had managed to cook
your *moujaddara*; you laughed,
said you had no doubt. Then I asked
if you remembered the times

Zeina Hashem Beck

I kept jumping from the top of the closet
on to the bed; how I was convinced I flew, if only
for a few seconds, and how you believed,
said *Yes* said *Good job* said *I see you.*

Mother, Ka'aba

I moan and the nurse reminds me, *The Prophet said heaven is under the feet
of mothers.*

When mothers give birth, the heaven under their feet is dark. *The first
milk, called colostrum, isn't white,* she explains, places the pump on my
breast.

*Your mother then your mother then your mother then your father, said the
Prophet,* says the nurse. She insists I change the feminine pads regularly.
Warm baths help.

The blood, the days – they don't stop. The pads irritate me. My husband
gives me his white cotton undershirts to cut and use instead. Each shirt, a
small offering. Each shirt, as white as milk, then dark.

The nurse tells me she missed her prayer rug after her first delivery. *Because
we can't pray until the bleeding stops.* She peels the tape off my skin to
remove the IV. She says mothers, too, are a kind of *Qiblah,* the direction in
which we all pray in the end.

She presses her thumb into my arm. Mothers, a kind of *Ka'aba.* Removes
the catheter. Final pilgrimage back to where we came from. Alcohol
pad, gauze. Mothers, a first temple. Give thanks, circle seven times,
counterclockwise. *Mabrook,* she smiles, *what a beautiful baby girl.*

Say Love Say God

I liked the idea of an impossible love.
I was told a love so different can't
make children with souls
worth praying for. But those stories
in the Bible and the Qur'an,
love, we knew what they meant.
When you said *sin*, love, you did not
mean my legs, or the way
you were already inside me.
When you said *sin*, you meant
how one forgets. Do you remember
how we slept naked? You were there.

I believed love is immortal, irrational,
and sometimes, tired. The sun, it seems, worships only
the bodies of the young. When I say *old*,
I mean how far we've traveled, love, how we go
back. When I walk new cities, I always
think of you, love. I tell you, *Look –*
lives upon lives upon lives.
Sometimes heaven is when I'm away from you, love.
Sometimes heaven is only the two of us. I know you
understand. Only petty loves want to be worshipped.

I liked the idea of an impossible god.
I was told a god so different can't
make children with souls
worth praying for. But those stories
in the Bible and the Qur'an,
god, we knew what they meant.
When you said *sin*, god, you did not
mean my legs, or the way
you were already inside me.
When you said *sin*, you meant
how one forgets. Do you remember
how we slept naked? You were there.

I believed god is immortal, irrational,
and sometimes, tired. The sun, it seems, worships only
the bodies of the young. When I say *old*,
I mean how far we've traveled, god, how we go
back. When I walk new cities, I always
think of you, god. I tell you, *Look* –
lives upon lives upon lives.
Sometimes heaven is when I'm away from you, god.
Sometimes heaven is only the two of us. I know you
understand. Only petty gods want to be worshipped.

There Was and How Much There Was

There was and how much there was.
Women gather in this living room.
They empty and fill the coffee cups.

>   I count the flowers on the curtains
>   when we ... I get bored.

>   Try oil. I like the glide
>   of our bodies in the night.

>   My friend's mother showed her
>   a video about it, the week before
>   she got married. I was still single,
>   and I asked. No one would tell.

The women laugh.
The walls don't have ears here.
Everybody is a woman here.
Some women bleed. Some don't.

>   Did you?

Every woman bleeds
one way or another.
I wear fewer clothes, less
hair on my body, and still
he doesn't. Where can I find
the sugar?

There was and how much there was.
All the women here love chocolate.

My first husband, he wanted me
to hide my arms, my legs, my laughter.
I told myself love means to change –
bullshit. I knew how much he loved
his money, so I flung his wallet
from the balcony. It opened its leather
wings and fell flat onto the street.
I told him I did it
because I hate long skirts.
I made sure my second husband
likes to drink and dance and carry me
on his shoulders in the middle of the club.

The woman in the blue dress starts singing.
The others clap, sway
their heads, their shoulders.
Ya salaam, Allah, Allah.

When I was a little girl, my mother
told me I was beautiful, but not as much
as her. I took her kohl pencil and drew
a mole on my left cheek. All I wanted
were lips, eyes, hair, hips, a smile
like Hind Rostom.

The women sigh.
Ah, Hind Rostom.
They have all seen *La Anam.*

I heard she refused a million
gineih offer to turn her life
into a drama series.
Oh what I wouldn't give.
Some bitch at the gym today
walks in, stands in front of me,
talks to my husband. Size 36 women
get away with everything.
Hind Rostom wasn't a size 36.
I shouldn't, really,
but pass the chocolate.

There was and how much there was.
One woman switches on the TV.
It's time for her Arabic-translated
Mexican show. Last episode.
Antonio is about to kill his brother
and marry Rachel.

Have you heard about Marwa?
Her husband took a second wife.
She keeps quiet because of the money.
The other day, I asked the sheikh
about Aisha, the prophet's wife.
I said, "Is it true she was often jealous
and once told him this God of his
only brings down *ayahs* convenient?"

One woman says she read that
somewhere. Or heard it.
Says marriage will make you say
strange things. Faith too.

The sheikh spent half an hour telling me
a story about honey and the Prophet's wives.
I forget what it was. When I kept asking,
he reminded me it was the rasool
we were talking about. I said, "But
wasn't he mortal?

And if he bathed too long
wouldn't the tips of his fingers
have shriveled up, like ours would?"

The women agree but advise her
to ask for forgiveness, nevertheless.

استغفر الله

Antonio has killed his brother.
Gun still in hand, he kisses Rachel.
The women change the channel.
There's an old Egyptian play.

    Oh keep that one. It cracks me up.
    This is Raya, this is Sakina.
    They are sisters who kill
    women and steal their jewellery.
    In the end, one kills her daughter
    without knowing it. Once she knows,
    the play turns tragic. My favorite kind.
    You laugh so much and in the end
    you cry and think where
    did this come from.

There was and how much there was.
One woman says she always cries
when she watches a movie on the airplane.

    It's so embarrassing but yes,
    every single time. Like when Diane Lane
    cheated on Richard Gere and I'm thinking,
    why am I crying? What's that got to do
    with me?

The women pass the nuts, the cheese.
Some drink orange juice, some wine.

    My fifteen-year-old son lectured me

about the wine the other day.
He said it was *haram*.
He asked why I've not gone
to Mecca with his father last year.
I said, "You know what
Allah says? He says,
Respect your mother."
I told him, "YOU came out
of ME. Shut up." I told him
all religion is metaphor.
He asked what's metaphor.

The women's laughter is louder.
One woman says no man
understands metaphor.

    Pass me that bottle, I need
    another drink. Sometimes I feel
    I should've aimed better
    when I flung my slipper at him
    when he was a child. Should've
    hit that head of his, knocked
    the stupid out of it.

There was and how much there was.
The woman with the black fringe
knows how to read the coffee cups.
The women say, "Please, please."

    I see a big white fish. It means
    money. I see a narrow wavy road.
    It means sickness, or perhaps
    bad news. This is the head of a bird
    here, its small beak. Perhaps you
    have a burden; it will be lifted,
    inshallah. Children are good,
    snakes are bad. You will travel.
    Lick your thumb and press it
    against the bottom of the cup.

I hope your print is white
like the sun. But don't listen
to me. This is just for fun.
Allah says fortune tellers lie,
even when they tell the truth.

The women light their cigarettes.
The men are playing cards somewhere,
the children are sleeping.

Last week, at the mall,
I was peeing and I heard
a woman tell her friend
her hair was falling out.
I started crying. My hair,
it's falling out too. I keep
a picture in my bag
of my graduation night.
Look, look how pretty
I was, how tiny my waist.

The women look. They tell her
she is beautiful. Her daughter
looks just like her, *smallah*.

My daughter fights with me
all the time. Nothing I do
makes her happy.
The other day I told her,
"You cow." I felt bad
five minutes later,
made myself some coffee.
I try to tell my husband,
but he blames me.
I prefer to mumble it all
to the kettle as it boils.

The women nod.
They yawn, they stretch.

20   Zeina Hashem Beck

Look how late it's getting.
This talking never ends.
We better leave before
your husband comes back home.
See you next week.

There was and how much there was.
Before they leave, the women
wrap the leftover cake
with aluminum foil.
They throw out the cigarettes, the ash.
They collect the empty glasses.

HERA LINDSAY BIRD

Hera Lindsay Bird is a poet from Wellington, New Zealand. Her debut, self titled collection, *Hera Lindsay Bird*, became a bestseller in her home country after her poems 'Monica Geller' and 'Keats is Dead So Fuck Me From Behind' went viral. *Hera Lindsay Bird* is published by Penguin UK. She won the 2017 Sarah Broom Prize and the Jesse Mckay Best First Poetry Book Award 2017, and was awarded a New Generation Arts Award in 2018. *Pamper Me to Hell & Back* was published as a Laureate's Choice in 2018.

My work is certainly influenced by US poets such as Chelsey Minnis, Mark Leidner, Kimmy Walters and Frank O'Hara, but I also takes inspiration from dead lesbians, comics and fiction writers around the world including P G Wodehouse, Elif Batuman, Patricia Lockwood, Chelsey Peretti, Tove Jansson, George Saunders, Lynda Barry, Shirley Jackson and all the Mitford sisters who weren't Nazis.

Currently I work as a children's bookseller, and my favourite books for kids are Harriet the Spy, The Mixed Up Files of Miss Basil E Frankweiler *and the* Moomintroll *series but also anything where a frog is a detective and solves crimes. In my spare time I re-read Agatha Christie & watch figure skating tournaments.*

Pamper Me To Hell & Back *was the result of a selection of poetry that won the 2017 Sarah Broom Prize – judged by Carol Ann Duffy. For now I'm trying to take a break from poetry and work on a couple of other projects.*

Bruce Willis you are the ghost

It's not that your wife doesn't love you. It's because you died and now
you're a ghost and she can't hear you talking to her. That time you saw
her taking off her wedding ring? It's because you're her dead husband
and she can't continue to mourn your absence with heterosexual
jewellery indefinitely. Stop haunting her already Bruce Willis! Bruce
Willis, it's hard to be a ghost and not know you are a ghost.
Haven't you noticed the only person you've talked to in a year is a
                                                    supernaturally
gifted child? Don't you think it's weird your wife just cries alone
in the living room every night, re-watching your wedding tape and never
looking or speaking to you? Don't you remember being fatally shot in
the stomach at the beginning of the movie? Walk towards the light,
Bruce Willis. Walk towards the light.

Speech time

*Four score and seven years ago our fathers brought forth on this continent, a new
nation, conceived in liberty, and dedicated to the proposition that all men
are created equal.*

That's how Abraham Lincoln started the Gettysburg address and he got
murdered in a theatre.
That's also how I have started my speech but I won't be murdered in a theatre
When I die, it will be an old-time injury, like falling into a threshing
                                                    machine.

I am always making speeches, but speeches are a waste of time
The only useful speech is one where you enumerate someone's many failures
until they burst into tears
But if anyone is bursting into tears today it will be me
I just want to lie naked on a deckchair, fanning myself with divorce papers

I have called this speech 'speech time' so you will know it's time for speeches.
Anything can be a speech if you say it out loud for long enough

This is not freedom of speech, this is just extreme oratorial leeway
It's hot piss, melting the toilet ice

Speeches exist for the purpose of making other people think what you think
But I don't want just *anyone* to be able to think what I think
It's like if paisley were a natural resource, and people had to mine for it
You have to be stupid enough to want to

I've been making a lot of speeches recently because I published a book
And more than a book people like to hear you talk about your book
People don't like books they like speeches
But not this speech ....

People don't want to hear poetry, they want to hear people talking about poetry
People don't want to hear poetry, they want to go home and not read poetry
and so do I
The only reason for poetry is to have a meadow in which to burn yourself
alive in
A picturesque meadow, with bonus violets

I am bored of making speeches
I have to say so many things I don't care about
It reminds me of life
It reminds me of when you are a cowboy and your hat gets too heavy

There is nothing in this world really worth saying
Being clever is a waste of time
I just want to sit around in Swarovski earrings and let old men debate my
literary merits
... but I don't even have my ears pierced

A speech is the opposite of a poem
A speech is telling people what to think, but I don't know what should
be thought
Sometimes it seems to me like other people aren't even trying to tell the truth
Like, when I watch porn I like it to be the retro kind when you can't see the
dick go in

Forget this speech, I'm changing the title
The new title of this speech is 'poem time' because this is poem time not
speech time
It's like when it's your first day as a soldier and you show up to the wrong war

Or like sexily cleaning the coliseum with a black feather duster
It's like panicking because your castle is too beautiful
Or an advent calendar for atheists full of empty windows
It's like pouring cold champagne all over your thighs
Or an evil piano that can only be played at midnight

A poem should never be a tourniquet
You have to let the blood goes where it wants
It's like trying to log into your email account but your password makes you
too sad
It's like Shakespeare .... etc

I love writing poetry because it gives me casket pleasure
I can feel my death somewhere far off
It's like doing a shot of semen after sex and calling it a chaser
Or when you're a ghost and can feel the wind blow in through your sheetholes

Poetry is like a tuxedo that zips off at the knee
It's my pet boredom ......
I sit in my room with the rain coming down
And I start to *wonder* about my life

Poetry is like pushing a pram through the dawn
But the pram is on fire, because the fire is your baby
It's like having an orgasm every time you hear middle C on a piano
Mozart is just elaborate foreplay to you

It's like upgrading your horse-drawn carriage to a better, more technologically
advanced horse drawn carriage
Or squeezing your mop into a tropical fish tank
It's like being the Monet of blow jobs .... and losing your boyfriend
to the Toulouse-Lautrec of blowjobs
Or a bedside drawer packed with snow

Poetry is a luxury behaviour
Like crying because you're too clever and nobody understands you
It's like cutting your hand at a party and referring to your blood
as 'party blood'
It's like: welcome to good behaviour town, population 0

I want to get high my whole life with you

i feel it in my leather hotpant pockets
i feel it in my anime wind blowing through an alpine tennis resort
overcome with wildflowers
i feel it in my ironic valley girl hairflip
i feel it in my admittedly limited knowledge of the Roman mythologies
i feel it in my biopic about a corrupt alcoholic educational resource salesman
advertising increasingly less and less educational resources
i want to get high my whole life with you
i feel it in my anime wind blowing through an alpine tennis resort
overcome with wildflowers AGAIN, and the poem isn't even halfway over yet
so what if my blood is the wind
so what if I love you so much I am becoming stupid
my heart melting like red candles on Satan's birthday cake

i want to get high with you out the back of our family funerals
i want to get high with you at an industrial carpet outlet store
i want to get high with you at the top of the Grand Canyon and pretend like you are
going to push me in and scream and pretend to try not to get pushed in even though
i know you pushing me in is the last thing you want because if you did that I'd die
and you don't want me to die
i love you so much I tell you about it
i love you so much I have already picked out my grave and written your name on it
when you laugh in the dark
it fills up the corners of the room with a thousand upside-down cartoon bats

how dare you be the kind of person I would immediately fall completely in love
        with and be devastated if you left
how dare you come and do that

your eyes
like two black cats
licking their assholes
in the hot morning sun of my face

O this feeling has drenched my bones
and turned my skeleton pink
with you I feel my mind changing
with you I feel my blood changing
i want to get really good at woodwork
i want to get really good at woodwork
and go into the forest
and cut up some logs
and make you a beautiful house to live in

I will already remember you for the rest of my life

Standing on your balcony in winter I think:
I will already remember you for the rest of my life
It's too late now, I know who you are
and what you look like
and must henceforth venture through life recalling you many times
as you continue to make things difficult by reminding yourself to me more
                                                              and more
by taking me to various locations and describing to me your ....
                                                    aspirations
some ancient moon smouldering above us
I will always think of you and how it was between us
and the things you did and said

I will think about your ... personality and your ... interests
and the specific colour of your hair and eyes
even if we have a terrific breakup and stop calling each other
I'll still remember you
I won't be able to help it! You're there in my memory
like the concept of opera. Or the Simpsons theme song

like a field of blossoms in an air freshener commercial
sarcastic with light
I will think of your temperament and your enthusiasms
and how you ... looked at me
I will think of all the things you told me about your life

I am so in love with you I want to lie down in the middle of a major public intersection and cry

is not how you are supposed to start love poems
but I'm too far gone
to work up to it gently

your naked back in the mirror
has cured at least 3-4 major diseases

for you, I would set myself on fire in a smoke detector factory
for you, I would ride through the mall on a Segway knocking juices out of the
hands of thirsty real estate agents

your lungs like Christmas stockings waiting for Santa to climb down the
chimney & put cancer in
your face like the face of a dead French revolutionary in an outdated
children's textbook
my stupid heart .... like a snowglobe .... filled with blood

If you left me, I would be forced to gaze despairingly into the middle distance
If you left me I would be forced to emotionally distance myself from the
situation as a self-preservation technique until eventually I healed enough to be
able to consider romantic relationships with other people, all the time secretly
resenting you for failing to sustain your attraction to me despite the totally
involuntary & uncontrollable nature of human desire

your teeth like a graveyard .... in springtime
your tongue like a mattress .... in a graveyard .... in springtime

your tongue on my cunt like a mattress .... in a graveyard .... in springtime
my pubic hair like the black carpet on the titanic
my ass .... like an ass buffet

you put me in a friendly but uncompromising headlock
you bite me all over my neck and shoulders

i don't know how to write a love poem
because love is indescribable
it's this feeling you get
when your mind gets hot
and everything else gets insignificant .... with diamonds on it
and you have to laugh and laugh at things in your second-hand dress

the slow rising of your eyelid
like a girl's skirt

my eyes like two envelopes stuffed with snow and no return address
my eyes like pair of pale blue cowboy boots walking slowly down a city street
towards you

it's like
you've finally found someone that interests you
and you get more and more interested
like a fascinating disease
it's like
for some reason, you have to think of the wild west all the time
but it doesn't make any sense???
because you don't really care about the wild west!!!!

it's better than TV
to look at someone and feel so much happiness
your smile a single arrow, quivering in a tree trunk

it's like .... life is not a punishment
and sometimes good things happen for no reason
I stare and stare at you like you were a distant mountain in a homeopathic
video game
with rare and medicinal flowers on it.

Watching six seasons of the Nanny while my long-term relationship slowly fell apart

Watching six seasons of the Nanny while my long-term relationship fell apart
Was more self-inflicted boredom than nostalgia
As Maxwell chased Fran up and down the staircase with a frying pan
And I lay in bed, listening to the distant sound of trains
Pulling their shit-for-brains cargo through the dark

There are some months when all art feels worthless
And life feels thin, and weak and full of spite
And the pastel hysteria of spring of outside the window
Just makes me wince with disappointment and rage
And the total, mind-numbing futility of it all
Often, I think about the man who walked into the National Gallery
And punched a hole straight into a ten million-dollar Monet painting
Of a sailboat, drifting down a river of autumn leaves
And got sent to prison for five years

There's nothing in this world more boring than heartbreak
It's like a tax audit of the soul
And what once seemed rare and poignant
And full of emotional promise
Just makes me want to dose myself to the brim with horse tranquilizers
And take a long vacation to skeleton town

There's only so much sitting by the window
Begging the moon for punishment
You can take, before you have to get mad
And stride up and down the toiletries aisles of the grocery store
Wishing every old woman painstakingly reading the back of a Listerine packet
An expedient journey to hell
And all the poets you loved
Reveal themselves to be little bitches
Whose constant need to reupholster their pain
Seems sad & extravagant
Like grief factories, polluting the local waterways with pathos and nuance

The present has overflowed and turned the whole past bad
Ancient Greece, art nouveau, the entire Italian renaissance
All ruined
Monet too, with his surfeit of waterlilies
Wilting in the heat like a loose-leaf salad

I sit like Nostradamus
In my kingdom of disappointment
Burning down the cities of the future
Going through my google calendar
listing all the bad things to come

DAVID BORROTT

David Borrott was born and grew up in Ilford, Essex. He has had numerous jobs (the best was fruit-picking) and travelled widely. He now lives in Lancashire with his partner and their three sons. He has an MA in Poetry from Manchester Metropolitan University. His poetry has been anthologised in *Watermark* by Flax Books and in *CAST: The Poetry Business Book of New Contemporary Poets* (Smith|Doorstop). In 2015 he received a New North Poets prize from The Northern Writers' Awards. *Porthole* was published as a Laureate's Choice in 2015.

If the brain is our hardware and language our software, then poems are not emails but programs meant to impinge on your operating system. They are patches or even malware; they tweak your consciousness to show you another view of things, to make them clear from a different angle. As Elizabeth Bishop says 'I was made at right angles to the world and I see it so. I can only see it so.' Or as Wallace Stevens pronounces, with his usual grandiose flourish, 'I am the necessary angel of earth, / Since, in my sight, you see the earth again, / Cleared of its stiff and stubborn, man-locked set.'

Poetry can be ameliorative. It can also be cathartic because, as Spinoza says, "Emotion, which is suffering, ceases to be suffering as soon as we form a clear and precise picture of it." Or, to end bathetically, sometimes poems are small adventures to go on, little trips, a three-minute YouTube video, drugless highs.

Narada

after a parable by Swami Vivekananda

So Narada said to sky-like Krishna,
'Lord, show me Maya,' as they left
the fertile land and entered an arid place;
sand, each grain unique, blew about their feet
and raced before them towards the west
where jagged mountains tore the skyline.
Krishna said 'I am thirsty, Narada, can you fetch me water?'
and Narada went but at the water fountain
he met Michelle from human resources
who was beautiful as the flight of birds
and she told him of a gig that evening
close by; so they went together
and for a pizza beforehand
which they both enjoyed tremendously
and Narada forgot his waiting master.
The next morning, he sold assurances
and bought futures and became a valuable asset
for the company. He and Michelle dated,
married, mortgaged a house and raised children.
So it was that 12 years later the dam
above their house burst and water gushed
through their upstairs bedroom. Narada
flailed in the flood, his children clinging
to his shoulders and Michelle beside him.
They swam towards safety when a surge swept him
under, he rose gagging and alone,
in tears he drifted to the crumbling bank
and there Krishna helped him to his feet.
'My child,' said his blue master, 'where is the water?
You have been gone for half an hour.'

Pigeons

I love the shiftings of my neighbour's pigeons
as they swirl a ragged loop above the houses
as if in a vortex or on a long string,
grey against the grey sky, orbiting
the coop where their owner drags
on his morning smoke and follows as we all do
the flex and oscillation of their flight.

It's the unification of the group that amazes me –
how each individual bird invents the flock
pulling together to become a spun set of dancers
stretching the edge of the turn or lifting
to redefine the cumulative angle, the joined geometry that
flouts the television aerials, muscles past the pines
in the conjugation of their joyful ellipse,

each giving way to the general pattern
to become something more than themselves –
a single swooping transport, of one spirit
flying, as words can ally in a crowd of words,
if just momentarily before the leader turns leaden,
the noose closes and each bird comes to earth
on that derelict shit stained hut that everybody hates.

Ultrasound

With four point five megahertz of clarity,
through jelly on your lifting bulge,
we see into our future: a prophecy
that flutters against your gut,
a resonance vaguely like ourselves.

For you, it is already here:
For me, it is as intangible as tomorrow,

as if far away, submersed amid oceanic depths,
a greening on the scope,
looming, rising on anticipation's winch.

Tonight I may place my hand
on the projection of your belly
and feel only a warmth,
as one feels casually on the bonnet of a car
that has been somewhere, has somewhere to go.

Self Portrait with Fiddling Death

After Arnold Böcklin

Death stands behind me fiddling,
by fiddling I mean playing the violin.
Death is his usual skeletal self,
imaginatively thin but a palpable symbol
and stark: the drumlins of his old skull,
the darkness flowing through his ribs.

The music fills the room like a fog,
it hangs in droplets from the furniture,
dampens my palette, muddies the paint.
His violin is curved like a scorpion's sting.
his bow cradles the bridge, drifting over
the strange ocean it is pulling in.

Surely he misses some notes his fing-
er-bones jar on the chords or pluck
an off string, but I know the tune anyway.
As the darkness behind us ferments
how similar we become, our open smiles,
after a while it's only the violin
that distinguishes us.

'felicitous blending of figure and landscape'

Two youths are fighting on the high street.
One with a logo of blood on his white shirt,
the other's fists are tight as apples;
a clench of excitement runs through the watching people,
their faces like a row of broken plates.
Dummies in the glass extend the crowd –
'Next' says the shop sign.

On the stone plinth of the war memorial,
a woman with XXXL breasts is smoking.
She rests earthmotherly on the steps.
Smoke rises around her like billowing hair,
or her own ghost filtering into being,
its intricacies merge with a sycamore
as she stands out against the monument.

A man is pissing down an alley.
It is night and a soft untroublesome rain persists.
Street lights reflect in the puddles,
touches of orange amongst the grey and brown.
His fawn jacket is darker at the shoulders,
his half-cocked trousers are shadowy, vague.
It is almost as if he hovered there on the jet of his stream.

Wolf Fell

You stand on the edge with your wife,
your balding head a wholesome colour
in the November sunshine. You are
taking a picture of Wolf Fell,
air-fuddled in the distance.

Here is the order in which these things shall be lost:
your remaining hair, the photograph, you, your wife,
this prominence, Wolf Fell, the air, the sunshine.

Southern Cross

Darkness and us moved high above the Pacific,
our 747 a corridor of stale air
swollen with the helium of sleep.
I dreamt a thousand miles and woke
to the window's stare, its coldness
crossing the glass to my hand, my eye.

The ocean below us dark as a fairy story,
a paradise of islands, forgotten boats,
of journeys under our journey, our hulking plane
a red flashing dot above their tilting masts,
and above me suddenly the stars, Crux unmistakable,
a neon welcome to the South.

Then a meteor charged the earth
slashing that constellation, Just for myself alone,
mouth widening to accept a wonder,
as if the sky had said yes, my reflected face
echoing the shock as that shining tick
ignites a hemisphere.

And knowing it was random – falling dust,
knowing outside it meant nothing; that meant nothing
to my keening head bursting with the fire of it.

Pigafetta and the Patagonians

After two months we saw a giant ten spans high
dancing, singing, throwing sand over his head
with yellow tattooed eye-patches, a red
ring skirting his face, white painted hair –
we gave him a mirror, he was terrified;
as we all are to see our true self clearly.

Here are seven facts about these folk
called Tehuelche or Aonikenk or Pathagoni.
1. Nomadic, they followed the guanaco herds across the pampas, living
only in tents made of guanaco hide.
2. Archers, their bows were strung with gut, their arrows tipped with flint,
tipped with poison.
3. When sick they dipped an arrow two feet down their gullet and vomited
a green spew.
4. A very agile race who do no harm. They were giants, so tall our tallest
barely made their waist. See also: de Weert, van Noort, Knivet, Faulkner
and Byron.
5. The women carry the possessions, loaded like asses, their breasts hang
down half a cubit.
6. At death, ten devils appear to dance around them and a greater devil,
most vigorous in his excitement, called Setebos. They paint themselves like
these devils.
7. They are now vanished into history, their successors overrun by cattle
ranchers spreading southwards from Fray Bentos.

They suited themselves with llama skins,
stuffed their boots with straw against the cold.
The Captain-General called them Bigfoot
and from this the whole region, Patagonia.
We tricked two, offering them irons
such as malefactors wear, these
they could not carry, their arms
being full of knick-knacks, so we clamped
them to their shins and caught them thus.
After that arrows were all their conversation.

One came as trophy on our vessel,
reciting the Hail Mary and kissing the cross –
he was the first to die in the Pacific.

And the eyes are other and the head is her
and the teeth are phor and the arm is mar
and the hand is cheni and the breast is ochii
and the penis is scachet and sex is johoi
and the buttocks are hoii and the heart is thol
(All these words are pronounced in the throat)
and gold is pelpeli and the sea is aro
and fire is ghialeme and water holi
and the stars are settere and the wind oni.

NATALIE BURDETT

Natalie Burdett is from the West Midlands, and divides her time between there and the North West. She is currently studying for a Creative Writing PhD, looking at urban place. Her poems have been published in magazines and anthologies including *A New Manchester Alphabet* and The Emma Press' *This is Not Your Final Form*, as well as being shortlisted for The London Magazine and Bridport Prizes. *Urban Drift* was published as a Laureate's Choice in 2018.

'Place' is complex and multi-faceted, providing sensory stimuli, containing our lives, and affecting 'perspective', so poetry of place is always in some way about the human experience. As I'm most comfortable in the city, that's a definite focus of my poetry, and I'm interested in celebrating but not romanticising the places that have had an impact on me. The title 'Urban Drift' refers to people being drawn to urban areas, while also referencing ideas of wandering within the city.

My favourite poets look outward – they are interested in their surroundings, and show us what it's like to be in the world. Roy Fisher once said, 'Like those of a spy / my words and actions have leaned to the oblique'. As a fellow West Midlander, I recognise a certain evasive or self-deprecating sensibility, particularly about our post-industrial landscapes. His poem 'Birmingham River' talks about towns and places I know well, but doesn't tell it straight.

The world's imperfect, but there's always hope and beauty too. It's easy to feel overwhelmed by increasing inequality and injustice and hard to ignore social and environmental issues, but even harder not to write poetry which has designs on us. I always enjoy getting a sense of something else going on under a poem's surface, and admire poets who see things clearly, but perhaps with a different lens, to use simple language in complex ways.

I'm not keen on sentimentality or nostalgia, and prefer down-to-earth realities of the material world, especially things that are seen as ordinary but, when you look closely, aren't. The world is worth taking seriously, and the poetry I go back to helps to remind me of that.

Baggeridge

1.

After heavy rain, water is trapped
near the surface by a layer of clay
red as a Staffordshire bull terrier,
collects in puddles of orangeade
then overflows them, streaming across fields,

cuts down through history
leaving tidemarks of black dust
on paths first cleared for coal trucks,
for open pits and deep mines
with seams that men could stand in.

Paths between Bag Pool,
Whites Wood and the Burning Field
have been relaid with slag
to open up the territory
for walkers, foragers, birders.

Wash away leaf litter, to show young soil
then red gravel and white grit,
then sand and, under that,
knuckles of hard core, half-buried
in the clay that sticks us to our bedrock.

Birmingham,

you're blossoming new curves. A warm glow skims
them, ribbons out across your city roofs
from Selfridges' bright aluminium discs,
to flick around the library's gold hoops.

At night a colder, more fluorescent sheen
accentuates your skyline's harder-edged
old towers. Polished steel casts well-built beams
of light which flash back from wet tarmac beds.

Inside the markets people claim a space.
Chermoula chicken couscous in deep bowls
steams up the glass; revives, illuminates
the dust-grey faces, highlights natural tones.

Outside, down low where nothing shines at all,
a sycamore seed sprouts against a wall.

The Soy Sauce Fish

Trapped, plastic body marked
not just with scales, fins, gills
but with a neat hook
at its capped mouth.

Doomed to be chucked
once empty – squeezed
for five seconds, crushed
and dropped to gutter-drift.

Lucky, it might float
bubble intact, spirit-level straight,
make its way back
to where the salt's external.

Why not re-fill the fish
with what you find delicious – let it live,
swim home, umami joyful,
sweet, salt, brackish, free.

Negative Spaces

An old man shuffles past a heap of bricks,
holding on one thin wrist a blue striped carrier,
eating a tray special mini-fish and chips.

Mortar foundation lines,
stretched out across tarmac,
chalk the corpse outline of a warehouse.

A weathered arch is crumbling;
grimy skin flakes off its bricks
exposing salmon-pink flesh.

A windowless former music hall
waits around for bulldozers, while dirt
in its guttering sustains a silver birch.

The underpass like a clean but empty fridge
steers us around the ziggurat –
peeled back to its spice-rack core.

A sky-blue fire exit ledge furs up,
collects litter, becoming more inviting
as new austerities and colder winds move in.

Bridges

1. Hulme Bridge

Bridge-building requires work. Draw plans, consider risks
then take a first leap into air. Reach out and up from each side
eleven cables stretched to hold the steel parabola.

The arc looks effortless far off, ties insubstantial, delicate
but up close on the bridge itself you'll admire
foundations, span and mass.

Each cable thick as two clasped hands,
bound to concrete with a bolt of two feet by two feet;
each strut a repaid trust that goes on hoping into the future.

2. Trinity Bridge

A bridge needs care; commit to maintenance.
Protect the structure linking two proud cities;
each has its own shadows, so keep the bridge well-lit.

Tend to paintwork, watch for rust – thick moss grows out of soot.
Put down salt on frosty days. Be clear on boundaries,
who will cut the grass, who cannot be involved.

Provide for romance: late night walks across the river,
early mornings on the bridge's curves. Try to see from both sides
where you're going, even when it's dark.

3. Oxford Road Footbridge

Bridge-breaking isn't tidy. There'll be diversions;
inconvenienced passers-by will have opinions.
Feel dust caught in the throat. Concrete will stain

44   Natalie Burdett

as cutting gear spills milk down surfaces. Break up hardware,
staunch wounds, see things previously held back.
Bind plastic sheets to scarred breeze block, chip board, plaster.

Wires will hang like weeds over blocked doors,
artery pipes cut at awkward angles. Hope in time for a clear view,
two smooth surfaces – detached, as if there never was a link.

Bobhowler

Crosses my room like a whip-flick then rolls, a grey Chinook
around the lamp. Too big for *moth*; its tremors take me back
thirty years to find my Grandad's word. I switch off the bulb,

but without glow it seeks heat, comes close slow-time,
low stealth-hum above my face. I slide under its buzz,
distract it with the landing light and shut the door quick.

Two words, distinct subtexts. That time we hung a sheet
on the back fence, used an outside lamp to call them to us,
we were unafraid – revelled in their glorious, mothy grace.

Blood

One sleeve rolled back
I sit, wait, looking the other way,
for the prickle, click, outflow
while she asks if it's still raining – she's good,
but puts the vials in my sight-line and it's dark,
almost black. They'll be sent off,
just hold my breath for two more weeks.

We meet half way
for a picnic and riverside walk.
Now our parents are tired, ready for home,
so I'm dropped off at the station,
and I have to jump out quick – there's no space to park.
No hugs. I wave, grinning hard,
but hurting as they drive away.

The South Wales train
has passed by lost coasts,
declining towns and industry to reach here,
and the wide window opposite
is smeared with animal blood – a cow was frightened
onto the tracks. I've missed my connection
and don't know what time I'll get back.

GERALDINE CLARKSON

Geraldine Clarkson lives in Warwickshire. Her poems have appeared widely in journals including *Poetry* and *The Poetry Review*, and in anthologies including *This Line is Not For Turning: An Anthology of British Prose Poetry* (Cinnamon Press, 2011), *Furies: A Poetry Anthology of Women Warriors* (For Books' Sake, 2014), *Best British Poetry* (Salt, 2014), *The Best New British and Irish Poets* (Eyewear Publishing, 2018), and *The Valley Press Anthology of British Prose Poetry* (Valley Press, 2019). They have also been broadcast on BBC Radio 3. She is a former winner of the Poetry London and Ambit competitions and her first poetry pamphlet, *Declare* (Shearsman Books, 2016), was a Poetry Book Society Pamphlet Choice. Supported by Arts Council England, she is preparing her first full-length collection. *Dora Incites the Sea-Scribbler to Lament* was published as a Laureate's Choice in 2016.

I grew up in the UK Midlands in a family of six boys and four girls. My mother and paternal grandmother were from the west of Ireland, which played a significant part in our growing up. My father was a barber and also did numerous other jobs, including working in several different factories, driving a taxi, and security work. His response to the sudden death from cancer of one of my brothers was to design and single-handedly build a house in Ireland in my brother's memory, learning construction basics from library books.

My father encouraged us all to develop our talents and since I was a compulsive writer he persuaded me to send off to magazines some of the stories I was writing as a child for my younger nephews and nieces, and I continued to write these for publication, along with articles, quizzes, puzzles, and songs, throughout my teenage years. This began to feel more formulaic than creative, however, and it was only after many desert years of not writing, including time spent in a monastic order where secular writing and reading were positively discouraged, that I began writing poems, thereby breaking the silence and reconnecting with the idea of writing for pleasure.

I find inspiration in exploring non-verbal art forms – fine art, sculpture, mime, and music – and enjoy collisions between poetry and other areas of life, collaborating with artists, athletes, scientists, actors and musicians, and writing across various media and in various formats – some of my poems have been 'published' on cupcakes and handkerchiefs, performed to diners at restaurant tables, and exhibited in public restrooms, at an airport, and on public transport.

Nuala, Nuala, Nightwatchman's Daughter

Nuanced at first, Nuala brutalised herself after seasons
in the cloister. The finer things belonged on the outside. Nothing
was as it seemed. Where she had envisaged a crucible of white-hot
smoking charity, was cold marble, clipped vowels, and salad bowls.

There was, however, work to be done. Scales of all kinds
to be dealt with – of fish, a glut every day in the kitchen; of tonic sol-fa,
to lubricate psalms in the chapel; of holiness, to which St Benedict assigned
seven degrees. In her blood was the waking gene, and like her father,

she would glide along dim corridors at night, checking for lights
and fires; blurting a word of solace to herself or some straggler,
alert to the closeness of danger, and of Death coughing his guts up
in the pre-dawn, his body under the blazing Sanctuary light, volted with pain.

Days Round like the Moon

Mapped to the urban (but the soul can live on a little green,
can thrive on a tree; witness Coleridge's patch of sky),
they nonetheless call themselves *women of the blue flowers*,
who flow back to the source, small and pink-breasted, multifoliate,
stamens alight. They will never be obsolete, women of the blue faces,
women of the blue fleeces, their tongues plumped up, giving rue,
dealing it like it was a winning hand at rummy, a many-wristed mother
wiping mouths of bambinos with a muslin napkin while thick white moths
gather at the door. During Compline on the radio, a husband makes a pass
at the agency cook, who takes it all in her athletic stride. At day's end,
the rhythm of the hours pauses on its cusp and the women reclothe
themselves in midnight blue, clutching the stars, women of the blue faeces,
dusting the moon and sinking down naked to dawn and Lauds.

'William lets me wear her ring –'

William lets me wear her ring –
a good brother, our two hearts caudate
and sheepshanked since babyhood.

A grab of gold and emerald
I take it to bed with me and stare at it
by candlelight till the sheen lures me in

and I figure in the greeny-yellow lick
her leaf-mould eyes – her thin waist –
her black rope of hair caught

like a noose on the neck
of an errant stallion –
her bell-voice calling out to

Billy, Billy, for help, but he's stepped aside
to visit with me and is saying, *Dear Sis,*
things will be as they were.

His voice, my own tones back to me,
freezes my *sang-froid*; cauterises
bobbing-girl gladness.

I put her back in the flame's eye
twenty-one times more, murmuring. I tell him
I had a dream and he lifts his soft face to me.

The thing about Grace and Laura

was that they were sisters, *vice versas.*
The gentleness of the one, tender
as mousse, flesh like marshmallow;
her demeanour like Turkish Delight;
an apricot, mooning at the sun.

The gunmetal slickness of the other,
her flick-knife wit and belt-buckle
tongue; operating from offices
in the City. I couldn't love
her. A wildcat, out of
control, she stalked me through winters.

Grace slides laughing on her birthday,
her velvet haunches streaked with yellow
from tiger lilies I've placed on her path.
Laura sucks in her cheeks and
intimates that, as per her email,
she won't be celebrating
anything in the current climate.

I edge away
from her coat-hanger glance.

If Grace and Laura were to marry,
that would be incest, anathema.
I covet a calling card for Grace
and she is always welcome.
Laura has me poked to bits
with reminders; red letters.

A Less than Sainted Summer

I can barely pull morning out of the bag,
come August. Our daughters have taken
to wearing serge uniforms
and folding blankets for a living.
The grandparents gurn at passers-by
from windows in their beach huts.
The weekend sunrise looks unconvincing
and there is no 'Oh!' in the ocean.
Uncles adamantly refuse to buy ice creams
for adorably-plaited god-daughters.

My future, a slim thing, languishes
on the leather sofa, with my past, locked
in gossip. My present – a perfect hostess
(puffing, dabbing at moist cleavage)
brings them steaming bronze tea,
shortbread angels, clotted cream eclairs.
A hardness in my heart rubs
against the bedroom furniture.
Vinegary flavours in my gullet
taint the milk. Vapours of aniseed,
elderflower, *Vapona*, link hands and skip.

I'd like to say that autumn was healing
but it was then that the dead leaves
stayed glued tight
and the house sweated tankfuls.

Miss Marple loosens her bra,

flicks dust and cottagey debris from the sill
and leans bare elbows through the lattice to catch
a snatch of South Downs air.

A line of sweat down her body's meridian
prickles in response to the breeze.
In the garden rock lilies stand to attention

and a low dog rolls cock-a-hoop in oak shade.
What path of peccadilloes led me here,
she wonders. Beyond the hills

the sea's serrated line seems years away
in the past, memories pickled like salt-kept
winter fish. She fingers a refolded

dearjane letter, always pressed to her person
only today her person seems the wrong
size and shape and there's a licking

restlessness, an itch to shrug off armadillo
shell and wriggle out from tiresome
chasing after clues, lascivious panting

at the door of others' misfortunes.
The grandmother clock strikes four-fifteen.
Miss Marple re-hooks herself

and chugs lavender talc
between her breasts. Cold cuts
and piccalilli, as usual, for tea.

Edwardiana

An inch or two skimmed from her twill skirt
and the day shaped perfectly in her head:
seamless tennis, swimming, a cycle down the lane
and up, rondeau of elevenses with aunts,
then two loops unhooked from her corset
for patriotic postprandial singing round the piano,
the map of England shaved perfectly on her head.
Strong tea in thin-lipped china, a cake-stand charged
with madeleines and buttered teabreads – mountains! –
shared perfectly by her bed: a long ramble
with a newish lover, in slant-lit gardens,
mallow weighting the air, and under row after row
of high-arching yew, yards and yards
of shadow waiting perfectly up ahead.

Dora Incites the Sea-Scribbler to Lament

Sees him at the far end of the strand,
squamous in rubbery weed, his knees bobbing
urchins, his lean trunk leaning, sea-treasure for her.

After it all (they mate, like carapaces, in parentheses),
Dora feels coolness in new places, lifts a reused
razor shell, mother-of-pearly and straight

and signals out to the swell of mouldering green.
Dora is electric, in love, and deep water.
Dora, Dora, Dora, in which dread is.

People people the beach, peering
through splayed hands, appealing:
DAW-RAAaargh. A boat sees her passing.

Sea-scribbler's chest buckles
in aftershock—his quill is primed:
squid-inked and witful.

Geraldine Clarkson   53

THIRZA CLOUT

Thirza Clout grew up in Kent and Wales and now lives on the English/Welsh border in Shropshire. For five years she chaired the Board of Wenlock Poetry Festival after careers in journalism, as a stand-up comedian and as a director for a conservation charity. In 2016 her first pamphlet, *The Bone Seeker*, was published by Mark Time Books UK and she won the Poetry Prize at the Doolin Literary Festival in County Clare. *Aunts Come Armed with Welsh Cakes* was published as a Laureate's Choice in 2019.

Instead of writing I sharpen pencils, play four-suit solitaire on my laptop, go for walks with the dog and generally fritter time away on anything but housework. My relationship with my mother was not easy when I was a child, but hats off to her – my sister and I were two of probably very few little girls at that time who were not allowed to do housework, because Mum and Dad firmly believed that homework and reading were more important. I like to quote a Fay Weldon character: 'The cleaner the house the angrier the woman'.

In one of my poems, 'January', I imagine burning the letters my father wrote to my mother before their marriage, which she kept. I am very glad I didn't actually do that, as the extraordinary story within them is inspiring my current work. I had kept the letters since my mother died in 1994 and it wasn't until I wrote the poem in January 2018 that I finally faced up to the need to read the letters – to deal with them and all the other boxes I hadn't even unpacked.

My first chapbook The Bone Seeker *was published by Australian poet Ross Donlon's Mark Time imprint in 2016. The central theme was sexual and physical abuse in my childhood. It was hard to read some of the poems from it in public – I felt sick with anxiety when I started to share them even with friends at a small writing group. However I was amazed at how many people sought me out after readings to say that they had felt I had written their stories, and this gave me the courage to continue and to publish.*

Aunts

Our family was lopsided, buoyed up on the bosoms
of plentiful aunts but near capsizing with such a weight
on Dad's side. Edie, Thirza, Ivy, Hilda nicknamed Hobbs
for her childhood crush on the cricketer, all were his sisters.

Glamorous Agnes whose beginnings Mother called bog-Irish,
poor put-upon Nelly who died young, his sisters-in-law;
Great Aunt Lizzie, who was very particular, was his Mam's sister.
Mother had two distant cousins she seldom saw.

Visiting aunts came armed with Welsh cakes, great tins full
(sugar, lard, flour, generous quantities of currants,
milk and egg to bind them, then browned on the bakestone).
A needy child I counted sleeps, longing for their arrival.

One time I saw my mother weeping on Thirza's shoulder
once overheard mother accusing all the aunts
of ruining me with too much love – her own legacy
she passed on: *spare the rod and spoil the child.*

She did not speak of the never-aunts Joan and Mary
whose infant deaths had left her an only child
nursing her parents cursing through old age. Henry
stumbling on crutches hobbled by arthritis and strong

Kent barley wine, blind Maud ten times hourly asking mother
to untangle her unfinished knitting, lead her to the outdoor privy.
Maud disappeared into the County Lunatic Asylum when I was five
I don't remember that anyone ever said to me how or when she died.

Breech

Twice she caught buses twenty miles to hospital
two hours each way with three changes
waiting on swollen feet at stops without seats
standing heavily in the heat of that July,
endured gloved invasions to swim me round.
She often told anyone how quickly I flipped back
kicking her womb as she carried her burdens home.
Especially she loved to emphasise how her waters broke
while she was serving groceries in the village shop.
Contrary from the start, that was her punchline.

I turned myself around to leave – headfirst I pushed
away from her. With her thumbprint she signed my navel
tenderly she pleated my newborn skin
taped on an old penny to mend the umbilical hernia.

Cousin Monica

Smoke rises into damp air at Pontypool Crem
as we park and try to recognise each other.
We don't mention her lung cancer or ask her kids
and almost adult grandkids to stub out their cigs.

Standing guard at the door her younger brother Dai,
dark suit failing to contain him and his grief, flails a punch
at Monica's son Dewi Bach, reconciled to her
beside her hospice bed but here still unforgiven.

Looking away the rest of us file in. Out of tune we cannot
scale Abide With Me nor banish Death's Dark Vale.
Amid our straining discords I think of Mon
mourn our silence, wish we had sung out together
those family secrets I suspect we shared
sung them out loud then cast them to the flames.

I am so sick of watching women die

I want Mimi to buy herself a pair of gloves
to warm her tiny frozen hands

I want Odette to kick Siegfried in the nuts
to break the stupid spell

I want Ophelia to jilt Hamlet and rule Denmark
after all the men finish killing each other

I want Hedda to get a job and enjoy multiple orgasms
with lots of lovers who are good to her

I want Emma to get an education and discover
marriage and poison are not her only options

I want Olga, Masha and Irina to laugh
and conquer Moscow – and Anna simply must

get custody of her son, ditch Vronsky
and join the Three Sisters' book group

I want to see living on stage and screen and page
women working, loving, women surviving

the streets are full

of slender people
body-con T-shirts
tucked
into belts
skinny jeans

they are laughing
sipping
skinny lattes
nibbling
pomegranate
seeds

they move
easily
along
narrow
pavements
cleared of fat
people

all we fat people are sitting at home
expecting a caller who will point a bony finger
expecting a caller who will tell us we are weighing down the world
a caller who will tell us we are time bombs of flesh primed to destroy the NHS
clinically obese guerrillas armed with knives and forks and spoons

we will put down our crisps and biscuits, our glasses of wine
lay down our diet books, our sugar-free colas and low-cal snacks
obediently we will follow the skeleton in the black hoodie

some of us are hoping he leads us to a promised land
all of us expect it will be filled with milk and honey

forty years

I love the way you take such pains
to mend broken things
apply superglue to fractured joints
handles of mugs we loved
cracked vases and jugs
you wash common geranium roots
free them from convolvulus
handle them tenderly as limbs
of the newborn babies
we could not have

forty years ago I loved the way
you never wanted to change your car
didn't care if moss
mottled the bonnet
passion stained the seats

I love the way we have transformed
blank space and concrete
a riot of roses scents the air
above tangles of nettles
rampaging ground elder

I love the pond we made crowded with newts
blue and yellow flags of iris, azure damsels
red darters, big striped dragonflies
helicoptering above water lilies
black cats pouncing from the shadows

in summer evenings we drank wine
listening to hooligan swifts, glimpsing bats
hunting from the church tower, breathing in
honeysuckle grown from cuttings leapfrogged
from Cornwall to Somerset to Shropshire

home from winter walks we shiver
turn away from our graveyard neighbours
stir up the fires to keep out frosts

The Bitterley Hoard

The farmer knows his land, thinks where soil is softest
in-bye pasture, the far ditch corner between two elms.
Behind closed shutters he listens to the night, his wife stirs
turns over, breathes evenly again. He takes the small brown tyg
fills it to the brim but not with drink, instead he pushes in
his leather purse stacked with coin. He creeps out, pads across the mud
pulls his shovel from the midden heap, hears a rustle, strains his eyes
catches the shadow of the old dog fox as it fades into the hedge.
He digs, lays down the tyg, covers it over, careful to leave no trace.

Satisfied he swills soil from his hands, joins his wife in sleep.
His treasure survives civil war and centuries of tilling, ploughs
broke off shards but still the tyg holds the purse, calf-skin soft,
his coins still safe. Hedge, ditch and farmhouse are faint lines
across landscape; the farmer and the fox have gone to earth.

LOUISE G COLE

Originally from Worcestershire but now living in Ireland, Louise G Cole writes poetry, short stories and flash fiction. She won the Hennessy Literary Award for Emerging Poetry in March 2018, and a Dublin pub was renamed in her honour. She performs at literary events in the west of Ireland. *Soft Touch* was published as a Laureate's Choice in 2019.

Poetry was always something other people did, and while I enjoyed listening and reading, I didn't write much of my own until later in life.

In my early 20s, as a keen hot-air balloonist, I was the editor of Aerostat, *a ballooning magazine, and married a balloon pilot before becoming one of the UK's youngest female newspaper editors. I then jumped ship into Press and PR, and was appointed Senior Press and PR Officer for the City of Birmingham.*

Fast forward a few years, during which time I wrote about and sold healing crystals and fossils, I was still working as a commercial wordsmith when we acquired an urge to emigrate from rural Worcestershire to rural Ireland. We landed in County Roscommon in 2003 with a herd of alpacas, two small children, two cats and a flock of laying hens, and began growing organic cabbages and salad leaves. I soon discovered mindless weeding and watering offered headspace for creative thought and after a while I began trying my hand at creative writing, mostly short stories and poetry.

I attend open mic sessions to practice reading my work aloud, and always enjoy interaction with an audience, especially when there is positive feedback. The gift of a namesake who models underwear is a great icebreaker at readings and a wonderful way for my name to be remembered. In Louise G Cole, the 'G' stands for Gillian, although I sometimes pretend it is for G-string, just to see if anyone's paying attention ...

Fur Coat and No Knickers

Drawing breath between tales of dead
      little brothers and elderly neighbours
moved away, my mother looks inside
      a lifetime that's 92 and counting,
claims no-one's visited for months,
      thinks I'm her cousin Betty
with designs on her fur coat and hopes
      of borrowing a fiver.
I try not to mind the care home smell
      and wonder what else to talk about when
the devil himself taps my shoulder
      suggests I unburden, reveal secrets
never before shared, so I offer a revelation:
      I lost my virginity four times
before I was married. She's never yet listened to me
      so it's no surprise she doesn't hear,
continues with a rattle about imagined walks
      in the park yesterday, shopping
trips she'll make next week.
      A carer comes to tuck her in,
brings weak tea and egg sandwiches,
      asks if I'd like some,
is relieved when I decline.
      I get up to leave and the frail old cripple
who used to be my mother
      spills her tea and demands
to know when cousin Betty intends returning
      the fur coat, says quietly: "I always knew
what a little whore you were."

Soft Touch

Stroking the navy-legginged thighs
of a woman who used to be me,
daydreaming at the traffic lights,
lost in the fabric feel of fantasy,

holding a freshly-minted
babe-in-arms, sleepy-wrapped
in a bunny print baby grow,
poppers snapped against wriggle;

leaning against the still-taut
muscles of a former six-pack
strained against stained singlet,
curled silver chest hair peeking;

embarrassed by smooth gussets,
newly-washed panties immodestly
teetering atop Monday's laundry
should-have-put-away-sooner pile;

hiding in a rock-chick T-shirt
faded into over-worn nightwear,
colourless soft cotton comforter
at bedtime's long, lonely stretch;

distracted by indecently tight
white boxers, clinging, I'm hot
blushing, not knowing where to
look, but I'm looking anyway;

or here's me, grey polishing cloths
formerly known as clothing, now
dusting shelves, mopping spills,
rubbing a shine onto mirrors

reflecting my life almost done.

Dirty Little Dresses

Back when you were still mine
– before school but after cradle –
we'd Wednesday walk to the village hall
puffing dragons' breath
across dim-lit benches and trestle tables,
our voices echoing bathroom-style.

At my feet, you spilled Dayglo orange squash
– the kind I wouldn't have in the house –
while I sipped something tepid and
vaguely coffee-flavoured from a plastic mug, tried
making big the small talk with other mothers.

All these years later I am surprised
at your recall of the precious poppet
pushed through the door, always dressed
in impossibly white cotton frocks, pretty, pristine
seldom up for finger painting and sandpitting.

She played quiet, solo games
emerging clean and unruffled,
remarked by a loud, proud parent
while you came back to me messy and wild,
hand painted, squashed and sandpapered.

You said you always had a thing
for her Snow Whiteness until secondary school
when she went Goth
and the dresses darkened to black,
full of salacious slashes revealing flashes
of snail-trail scars on pale flesh.

Neither of us heard what became
of the pushy mother.

Watermarked

The teeming river's upright heron casts
my father: alert, slim and spike-beaked
beady-eyed in two-tone grey, topped
with a slick, black-backed comb over
feathers presented neat, formal, unruffled

observing life and love, respecting fast water
watching calmly without comment.
Unspoken childhood hardships shaped
a quiet man, stoic, strengths hidden
in patience, reserve, attention to detail

small pleasures in unusual pastimes
ships in bottles, keeping bees, Austin Sevens,
high flying kites of his own making.
Like the heron, solemn, straight and steady
taking flight only when required, just for me

on days when needy, rattled, hopeless
I catch his unexpected shape overhead,
majestic wing-beat recalling that special day
when through a single thought, so intense
with longing, need manifested a grey heron

waiting on the gatepost, regarding my arrival
with a stern look, inscrutable, but so familiar
composed, sombre, self-contained, concerned
watching calmly without comment,
I saluted, was sure I saw him almost smile.

Worcester, as in Source

My sense of place still smells of Lea and Perrins
where I bore my children, two dead, two alive,
in the faithful city as tea time swans gathered
for bread shop buns, stale cakes, in the shadow
of the Cathedral, King John's thumb bone still
there in a much-fingered casket, bells loud
above willow-whack-leather of the cricket pitch.

Further along the Severn, Pitchcroft Racecourse,
when not under winter water, good for walks
or picnics, regattas or hot air balloons sailing
into a future where down and outs in shop
doorways watch fragrant ladies who lunch
order artisan-baked petit fours and canapés
for exclusive, after race, off-your-face parties.

Naming Petrichor

Not only scent, it has colour too, slate grey
like the rain it follows, shaded vague, pastel,
puddled, brighter in moonshine, transparent
in sun, more intense than yellow-green grass
or crimson crimped flowers – and a taste,
flavoursome, pungent, at once sweet and sharp.
Sound as well, steady, ready drips dropped
deliberately, soaked earth channelling watery
overflows into streams, rivers, lakes and an
ocean separated by boasts of its own salty
lexicon, while inland, we taste that air after rain,
see it, feel it, hear it, know the special smell
is different in one place to another, yet same,
name brought from a need to label life, love,
hope in the '60s, when anything was possible
but fifty years on, I fret over what we called it

before then? We knew it, loved it, dedicated
poems to its form before ever it was titled.
Until I can award a new name in recognition
of majesty, the tingle it elicits, senses slewed
sideways by its fleeting perfumed promise,
until then, it is petrichor. Petrichor, petrichor.

Growing Boobs

At the deli counter in Woolworths
I dreaded the little grey pervy bloke
who came every Saturday morning

to hold my gaze with a leer, ask for
exactly seven and a half ounces
of mature farmhouse cheddar

that's what they weigh, he'd say
staring at my teenage chest as I
positioned the cheese-wire, *each*,

and I'd hurry to greaseproof wrap,
take the money without touching.
He was ahead of his time, balls of

buffalo mozzarella more suggestive,
but they hadn't yet landed in rural
Worcestershire, this was the 1970s

where we also went without broccoli,
seedless satsumas, bottled water,
duvets, skimmed milk in cartons.

I was told not to mind, take no notice,
be respectful, poor man was probably
a war hero.

EMILY COTTERILL

Emily Cotterill grew up in Alfreton, Derbyshire and now lives in Cardiff. She works in the place management sector and is currently attempting to install poetry (not hers) as public art in central Cardiff. Her poetry frequently focuses on both leaving and returning to home and the moulding effect that a specific place has on a person. She suspects that this is inspired by the fact that when she first went to university she was convinced she didn't have an accent – it's an idea that she now finds hilarious. *The Day of the Flying Ants* was published as a Laureate's Choice in 2019.

My earliest memories of reading or listening to poetry include Spike Milligan's 'On The Ning Nang Nong' and the nonsense verse of Mervyn Peake. I came to serious contemporary poetry as a teenager through the surprisingly diverse second-hand selection in Alfreton's many charity shops where I also picked up such formative classics as The Autobiography of Malcolm X *and* The Empire of the Sun *as well as through an A Level English teacher who encouraged me to read out the more explicit parts of Tony Harrison's 'V' to the class.*

As a child I always wanted to be an author without doing much about it, but I vividly remember writing my first 'proper' poem. I was 10 and in my bedroom looking through a free Christmas magazine from Tesco when a poem that I called 'Gone' appeared in my head. Not long after that I went on a school trip to the Magna science centre in Rotherham, which used to be a working steel mill. When we got back to school we had to write a poem about the trip and thinking about it now the poem I wrote (which I still remember word for word) was actually about the inherent melancholy of deindustrialisation. I suppose I haven't moved on much since.

At Least Not in Wales

after R. S. Thomas

Come on, and move back west with me.
The bright girls from the valleys will say
they can't hear the difference in English accents,
I won't know if they are lying, but I'll laugh.
Maybe in Cymru we can match – until I split myself
down an unforgettable seam, to show them
coal dust in my lungs, blackened blood matching theirs,
the threat of a red brick still hanging in the air.
England forces itself between each of us
and you cannot live in the present.

The Day of the Flying Ants

When did we learn that flying ants are not another species, just another sex?

I saw us twice today while the air was thick with wing beats:
once we were children, chlorine fresh from swimming
waiting on leisure centre steps, the other teenagers,
kissing loudly with wet mouths and worried hands.

On the day the ants fly I miss our possibilities most,
remember them crawling on our bare legs?

Somewhere new queens are making their nests and that reminds me,
I should have had you, terrified, while your mum folded sheets on the
landing.

In Mablethorpe

All the pubs have two rooms: lounge bar and a saloon,
with plastic chairs and smoke hanging dense in unlocked air.
Our man comes back from the bar, decants two sickly red VKs
into empty tuck shop cherryades and we've cracked it –
underage drinking with a white screw-top lid on it.

A square patch of foyer between the doors and
an old fag machine, kids slipping in for Camel Lights.
The bright music trivia touch screen and men
shouting answers about The Jam you knew for yourself.

On warm nights in the Midlands we drive right out to smell the sea.
The bone cold lingering from school nights on the same streets lifts
from the scabbed skin of our forearms. We pluck salt from the air
for our new wounds. The morning after we drive down the coast road,
clutch our sick stomachs and fly, just to see what comes from the hell of it.

The Cheeseburger Love Song

At the window is a woman you have loved against your diet,
gorged on the look of her with the guiltiest parts of hunger.
Her deft hands dance on the wax wrap paper, forearms
flecked with a hundred spitting oil scars. The fast food tattoo.
She is always here, and you suppose that she remembers you,
from her un-kissed acne years and all the warm paper bags between.
You, who would surrender your torso to the drive-thru window,
to take her by the over-washed polo-shirt collar and have her.
Her lips would have the cherry pink taste of market-stall gloss,
her mouth drenched in free-fills of fountain cola, and the thing is,
she has seen you, all of your faces in your repeated flash cars and
she could make you in a minute. Plunge your heart and her hand
into the deep fat, feel nothing. You are ruined, crisp and bubbling.
She scrunches your wrapping. She throws you away.

I Have Loved Coal

Like a teenage girl loves an older guitarist
with a rough black smudge of eyeliner.
I have built my life on it,
screamed down decades for it,
COAL NOT DOLE – bared my whole soul for it
but old women gossip about the pit,
I know the world has had enough of it.

Coal – with its head full of history,
strong arms, filthy engines, heavy,
the small town sex of it.
Broken bodies, white knuckle wives,
the silence of canaries – has risen
from slag heaps and pit heads to thick air
spluttering into anyone born
late with an old miner's lungs.

I have loved coal but recently,
when I sit in the fresh place built
on the scar of my grandfather's pit,
I have loved birdsong, greenspace,
the safety and hope of it –
wind turbines, rising white beacons,
sharp armed, slicing clean paths
to a future.

Joy

Fora while they peeled the new skin from the slag heaps by junction 28,
set machines to what men of a motion lost to our past couldn't muster,
picked out fresh coal from the cast-offs. they did not let us heal.
It's hard to remember if by then they had put up the noise protecting fence,
blocking the sight of Pinxton and the corrugated walls of Joy Mining Machinery
welcoming me almost home, next to the spot where, in the slack season,
travellers stopped: rocked up at school with the rough glamour of strangers.
Either way – on the way back from homes elsewhere I picture those diggers,
working out the last cash from our landscape. I hope someone has stoked the fire,
my wipers twitch in anticipation of rain. There are grey skies, hard work undone
in the memories of this place all that time spent travelling has made me make up.

'Bindi'

At the beginning of Brownies in the bowls hall,
I sit opposite Charlotte in the misshapen circle of
small white girls with culottes and crossed legs.
She has pressed a diamante sticker into the centre
of her forehead, as we pass the news around she calls it
a bindi. The real ones, she says, are pressed in with a pin.
She is two years older, I have no reason not to believe her.
In my bedroom is a Minnie Mouse pin badge with
a rubber butterfly back, sometimes I press it into
the soft skin inside my nose, jealous of boys who duck out
of lessons with blood dripping onto their wobbling teeth.
People do these things. That night, instead, I put it flush
to the flat bone above my nose, mark out a monobrow
from this excessively Western memorabilia, marvel
at the might of these new warlike women. I fear them.

West

It's best to re-enter Wales at dusk. Avoid The Bridge.
Dive from the Midlands into Monmouth and at the *croeso*
wind down your window, play *Motorcycle Emptiness*
to the famous air. Drive fast on the green roads,
they have little need for motorways just there.
Now gather what the English call consonants.
Cast off these new Latin vowels. Steady yourself.
If you must take the M4 into Cardiff, go slow,
mention the red trees smothering hillsides,
to the empty passenger seat, better yet, head west,
worrying the shape of the country until you find the sea.
Rain will fall in the mountains, and meet you there by morning.

NICHOLA DEANE

Nichola Deane was born in Bolton in 1973. She was educated at the Universities of St Andrews and Manchester. In 2012, her first pamphlet *My Moriarty* won the Flarestack Poetry Pamphlet Prize, and was a PBS Pamphlet Choice. Her work has appeared in magazines such as *Poetry London*, *Magma*, *Archipelago* and *The Rialto*. 'Yesterday's Child' was Highly Commended in the 2014 Forward Prize. Her first collection, *Cuckoo*, was published by V. Press in 2019. *Trieste* was published as a Laureate's Choice in 2015.

Writing is listening. If I am in a receptive state, of real listening, the poems come. But listening requires huge amounts of energy and stamina; it requires the whole body as well as the cogs and levers of the mind. It's not easy to listen. It's a radical letting go, until there is just the sound of the line, floating in mental space like Hamlet's father: 'tis here, 'tis here, 'tis (if you don't grab your pen in time) gone.'

One of the times when I feel I can let go a bit more, when I am less anxious and distracted, is late at night, and so quite often my poems begin then, just before sleep and when I'm reading poetry. When it gets a bit hypnogogic or trance-y. Wasn't it Michael Donaghy who said that poems come from next to nothing? It's like capturing butterflies in flight – you know, the tiny blue ones so rare these days that you think you've merely hallucinated them? – unharmed, with your bare hands.

The first hazy version of a poem will go into an A5 notebook. Sometimes a second or third draft. But mostly I'll switch to the computer pretty quickly, partly because my official writing time is very limited (childcare, my teaching job) and partly because word-processing helps me to sense (see-hear) line-lengths, stanza forms etc.

I listen to poetry a great deal, either to CDs from my collection (Merrill, Charles Wright, Olds, Muldoon, Jamie, etc) or to Youtube recordings and lectures (Bishop, Ryan, etc) as a way of 'deep reading-listening' whilst driving or doing domestic things such as cooking and cleaning the loo. I'm always trying to learn by heart that way, knowing that poetry dissolves the western distinction between heart and head, thought and gut. I've begun to learn that I don't write any of my poems, especially the better ones. If I am in a receptive state, of real listening, the poems come. But from where? The storm, sometimes, that Rilke sensed? The crackling air before. The deeper freshness after. Or sickness, dullness, the precipice of sleep?

Bowl

Drink and be whole again beyond confusion.
— Robert Frost

Or wood or bone or mud or plastic or silver,
with a family tree as long as history,
what are you, split-skull? What don't you know?
If we've forged an axe, we've dreamed a bowl,
if we've made a fire we've made you a home
for food, for bread (a womb for bread) for wine
and water and milk-into-wine. But what are you for
if not for everything? O room for absence

open to the sky! A home but not a roof.
We might say: a love without its shelter.
You place no seal on your pure hollow of praise –
praising's tomb. And if dust touches you
it sleeps in an eyelid bed, in half a world
singing lullay: *be here be whole be gone.*

Three Shades of Black

Here! Clothe yourself completely in swathes
of Lorca black, better to absorb the noonday sun.
Or strip to enter this flinty Dunkeld

burn, troubled with its own brightness,
weaving and wilding its black snow-water,
yet beading clear on the swimmer's skin.

Either way you'll end as you must: *a-cold,*
burning – starless black, Rothko-black,
dense, mineral, on black ground.

Portrait of Georg Trakl

after a drypoint by Milein Cosman

I have closed your book long since
but you're still staring your howl at me
from the locked ward of its pages.

Your eyes will not be walled up in that white.

The marks on that sketch are blurred in
left to right, as if, bridling, you'd just
jerked your head, mid-glare.

Under the recess of your brows is a long drop.

And I think of the one my father told me of,
the time he'd lain at the lip of the flooded quarry
and lowered the longest line he could

– butcher's string or a ball of twine –

weighted at the end with a stone adze
into the black water. Down it dropped
and down until he held the string by its tip

as it shuddered in the depths like a distressed pendulum.

L'Estartit

my father in Catalonia, 1961

'Careful.' The barman jerked his head
a little towards the closing door,
thumping, as if punch-drunk, on its hinges.

'Careful, *senyor*. Special Police. *Guardia
Civil –*' and, stepping back from his gaze
again, carried on revolving and polishing,

revolving and polishing, with plain white
linen, a clean, warm brandy balloon
so that there would soon be

no hint of fingerprint (those telling
whorls and loops like Celtic beasts)
no cloudy planets of human grease

on its surface when he raised it,
a breathed-on, empty chalice, up
to the one small source of natural light.

Yesterday's Child

Sorrow and rage, rage and sorrow
are beads on a thread of ragged prayer

and yesterday's child can't cut the string
and her life is strung on thin thin air

she knowingly doggedly sowing tomorrow
with sorrow and rage and rage and sorrow

Fig Ghazal

I am ghazal.
I am ghazal in the way that split fig
is split fig, and ripeness ripeness,
ghazal in knowing no other.

All is ghazal
and for the women
in their world-purdah,
with their force, drift, thrift,
make-shine, ache-shift,
their time-signature, I sing it, this

my body, the poured-out song you hear
muffled on the other side of the locked door.

Cityscape with Invisible Dog
after a remark by Donald Justice

My dog is in the poem though he isn't mentioned.
He trails along behind me in my sadness,
his leash not quite at full stretch, working
his nose up and down the regularly spaced
lampposts, squeezing his nostrils like a concertina.
You will not hear these inhalations in the poem:
the dog is in the rain but a different rain
which soaks him but is otherwise no tribulation.
Rain he does not howl at or invest with feeling
and when he lifts his leg in graceful attitude
it is to make a delible stink in the world.

Coming out of the lake into a big towel and her arms
after lines by Anne Carson

When the mother opens her arms to her child, the corners of the towel
in either hand, what is it that moves me further, deeper?
                                                The thought of my running
to some such embrace, the great imprecise blur of running and memory,
(not a lake but a bay, day's end, and the warmth, the double warmth
of cloth and arms, her spilling smile and running that way to my mother –
to be her smile or that smile's excess –)

or
                    the thought of either of my sons doing the same
                                            and that face that was hardly hers
coming into my face like a sunset, breaking my love
                                        right down to its colours,
my face dissolving, then, into the bass of all feeling,
night welling in my face, dissolving, reaching the root of every love?

Thanked Be Fortune

this breath escapes
what mind cannot
to
                    – changed air –

– charged sky –

Trieste

Our thin futon mattress on loose parquet,
white sheets, the sanctus of our skin.
Then light wakes me early.

                A coolness, doves.

Morning comes like a proof,
grief-balancing two hearts, where what's
between them is held like the bubble in a spirit level.

Crooked, violable is the way of the angel,

                    a candescent road.

Later we'll lark in the tideless winter sea
then turn our faces back to the sky to find it
carbon, dark as the lord of hosts.

                  All those sceptres of lightning.
Here, a few miles down the coast from Duino,
Rilke's shade still asks the sea wind
'What is coming? What approaches?'

And weather, like a Spartan messenger,

                  runs in, breathless

JOHN FENNELLY

John Fennelly, born in London to Irish parents, currently lives in Manchester, where he completed an MA in Creative Writing at MMU's Writing School. He is a poet, teacher, teacher trainer and poetry workshop facilitator. His work has been published in *The Long White Thread of Words – Poems for John Berger* (Smokestack, 2016), *One for the Road* (Smith|Doorstop, 2017) and commended in the Bridport and Bare Fiction Prizes. In 2016 he co-founded Black Cat Poets. He regularly performs at events in London, Manchester and elsewhere. He currently works as House Poet at MMU's Writing School, is working on a translation project with the Czech artist/poet Timo and a new collection. *Another Hunger* was published as a Laureate's Choice in 2018.

When I try to make some link between the poems I go back to, that I love and were/are portals discovery for me, the words 'integrity' and 'authenticity' come to mind. That sounds a bit grand perhaps, but I don't mean them as moral judgements, rather as explanations for a poem's emotional, aesthetic or intellectual impact on me.

Neither do I mean a preference for the confessional poem, or authentic and honest in the sense of being only linked to the lived experience of the poet. The biography may be of interest but what matters is the poem itself and the corpus of work in which it exists. The integrity of utterance and the fidelity to a hard won or sought for form, if only true to itself and the world(s) it creates, makes a poem that communicates itself as 'true' to the reader or listener. The authenticity as a created object on the page, or in the ear, is linked to that of 'integrity' in the Latin etymology of being 'whole', 'sound', 'pure' and 'complete', with 'authentic' coming from the Greek authentikos: *'genuine', 'original' and 'principal'.*

Chaser

Mum sent me to fetch at least a score
before you frittered
all your wages in pub or bookie,

and I found you in The Fellowship,
Sweet Afton smoke, navvy's boots,
neatly sculpting ruffs
round emptied pints of porter.

Holes, roads, tube lines
you dug and drank, I swore
you'd never see me travel.

Listening to the bodhrán
of rain over London, now I crawl
the craic through East End pubs,
Grave Maurice, Blind Beggar,
Hung, Drawn and Quart'ed,

still searching, with my map
of London's Lost Rivers,
draught and redrafts on my lips
an overdraft in my pocket.
But in yours, betting slips.
Crafty dead cert smiles.

And while I haunt these places
still alive, I find I am more
of a gambling man,
Dad, than I bet you'd ever have guessed.

The Present

We had gone to the barn on Boxing Day
pushing the door on cow quiet and dark.
A shape swung in the winter we'd let in
and wee Evie ran towards him laughing,
tiptoeing to reach the soles of his shoes.

Uncle Sean really could do anything
and walking on air, this was a new game,
necktie face pulling, hanging from a beam.
Then she was silent like looking up
to a crucifix. Sucked her thumb. Sought my eyes

that hadn't seen him wear a suit before.
Even on Sundays. Now he would wear one
always, like Grandad, when they laid him out
to wake and I was her age. Men standing
outside, black tied, *sorry for your trouble,*

which must have been to lose this choking stone
in my chest, kept steadfast, hard held promise
to make me a man you'd never see cry.
Hands, spat on for work, a clout or shaken deals,
lift ink-black pints that contract the tongue to silence.

Eucharist

Thankful, though its cool, wild dark invited,
I played statue and would not run on
with the other children to the hide and seek woods,
all bramble, thorn, nettle and velvet moss.

Siobhan had told me how babies were made:
a powder from what boys have, that girls don't.

And with that, she slipped her hand in my pocket
to pinch my last Flying Saucer full of sherbet.
I would have been eleven, hot-cheek astonished,
in love with her skipping off laughing with my sweet,
who would soon, *fruit of thy womb*, magic babies.
It was Our Lady's Primary last summer visit

to the Isle of Wight and, from time to time, I think
I am still entranced there in the long grass
leading from the cliff top to the kiss-chase copse,
the rice paper melting on her tongue.

My Father's Glass Eye

I

After seven operations failed
to reignite the real one, he came home with three,
two of polymethyl resins, lifelike
silk veins and iris indecisive blue
or green. His spare would stare
from the mantlepiece
so we'd always catch it,
his eye of providence.

Or later down the Irish Club
he'd place his Sunday Best
next to his stout,
I'm keeping my eye on you.

II

Lost navvying the Jubilee Line,
impaled on some thorn of steel
to a fascinating absence: glimpsed
satin behind a smooth curtain of skin
whenever he'd sleight it out or in.

Relishing this, especially on buses,
his motorbike sold. Index finger inserted,
he'd then pop it in his mouth
suck briefly its lozenge, give it a wipe
then deftly lift the tear thirsty flap
and pop it back.

At night, drink taken,
he'd often forget to take it out
and be found in the living room,
a snoring barrel of black,
iris enfolded back to read his dreams,
its white disc staring like the moon.

III

My lips on his cold forehead. Both eyes
finally closed. Undertaker's lies.

IV

I picture the green glass eye
is soon stilled to balance
on its cornea fulcrum
in the bowl of the skull
the pupil fixed
to scan the fathomless dark.
Above, the émigré trains flash past.

Road of Spoons

After watching Lanzmann's Shoah

There's a lake at the centre of Europe,
waters lapping shores of ash.

A disused train line, winter trees
and what were thought leaves, in black and white,

become, close-up, thousands of spoons
or tens of thousands, between tracks

that scrape to cold horizons. That oval
held by a mother, teased

her weaning child's mouth to a tunnel,
this, a last meal, or was lifted by bride

and groom to the other's lips
once at a wedding feast. Or these, handles

becoming menorahs or mirrors, sharper than knives.
At night each spoon's scratched whirl,

a miniature lake, gives back full
a sky's scarred bowl.

Another Hunger, 30th August, 2013

And there I was, a weeping head
pressed against the architrave
on hearing he'd died that day.

Not one gassed child in Syria
had induced a tear,
but he, my lachrymator
and there were many more
than one for every year.
Just another bloody gasman.

But I am afraid. Very afraid,
knowing a boy somewhere
will wrap around a bomb

to make the dead air
a moment's blizzard of blood and bone
or a girl point blank in the head, going to school,

that the loving as the unloved
have nothing to lose.
That poetry makes nothing happen

but to mind the tongue, éist the mouth
for a voice of glacier melt and scree.
Only turf grass bows to the wind,

and in the rain pelting the Brough,
blade and leaf flicker with each drop
as night gathers to drench us.

Snow

Furred rain, turned down to silence, layers soft
flurries down light flues in thrilling cold spells
of ice bling, jacked from the dark and flung as frost
for arms and legs to crick and print to angels.

Improbable manna of distant stars
dance, unique as loves or lives. What were the odds?
Gravity in time does for them on streets, parks, cars—
that blank to the stares of poker faced gods

at our numb fingered panic, which is just
to hi-five time aloft like nudged balloons—
for avalanche has to, as black ice must.
Like sleet on tongues our thousand or so moons,

the skid, the smothering, even this sonnet
a page turned to white, silent, infinite.

Those Flowers

I

I caught him yesterday, my younger self,
drinking Guinness, reading a book.
He followed me, hang dog
to at least two other pubs
before I had the nerve to ask
What the fuck is going on?
He tried that 'old man I know thee not'
but I saw right through him,
the sanctimonious, love-sick little shit.
You'll end up like me, I kept shouting
in my distress, till the police were called
and I was half-nelsoned into the ambulance.

II

This fella, who looked like my dad,
lost it in the pub last night.
He'd bought me a pint
seemed all right. Picking
up my copy of Heaney, he turned.
Said he still loved me
and how little time there was,
but I'd be his forever, how he could
never leave me. When he started shouting
Never send those flowers
in my face, fists clenched
on my lapels, *or you'll end up like me!*
It was then the barman called the police
who arrived with the ambulance.

VICTORIA GATEHOUSE

Victoria Gatehouse lives in West Yorkshire, has an MA in Poetry from Manchester Metropolitan University and a day job in medical research. Her poems have been published in numerous magazines and anthologies including *The North*, *Poetry News*, *The Rialto*, *Magma*, *Mslexia*, *She is Fierce* and *Poetry Salzburg Review*. Competition wins include Ikley, Otley and PENfro and she has been placed in many more. Her first pamphlet, *Light After Light*, is published by Valley Press. *The Mechanics of Love* was published as a Laureate's Choice in 2019.

I started writing at a young age, scribbling poems and stories at the kitchen table after school. In my teens, I decided to study biochemistry at university, leading to a career in medical research. I wanted to 'find a cure' for diseases, however writing was always my secret passion and I was an avid reader of poets such as Plath, Duffy and Olds. I kept notebooks and diaries in which I could express my creativity and this was something I kept in the background until my 30s, when I started to take my writing seriously and enrolled on an MA.

I've been helped along the way by the support of university tutors and also by some very generous and encouraging writing groups. Poetry is a passion that I have learned to keep in my life by adapting my working hours to allow time and space to read, write and attend spoken word events. I believe my scientific background does, at times, inform my work and this is a connection I would like to explore further.

The Mechanics Of Love

It ticks me to sleep,
the titanium valve in your heart,

so close, my lips could press
a gleam down the horizontal scar

where they opened you up,
hooked cannulised veins

to the heart-lung machine.
This room of ours, all soft

darkness until a car passes;
in the place where curtains

don't quite meet, a spill
of light, making me think

of that imperfect seal,
how blood streaked back

from ventricle to atrium,
more turbulent with every year.

Now, the deep red
chambers of your heart, secured

against the leak and tonight,
every night, in that pause

between beats –
titanium, titanium,

for its strength, durability,
its resistance to corrosion,

for this love, for those two
shining leaflets

clicking in their frame,
hinging on it.

Sixth Form Science Technician

The biology teacher wanted blood,
more than the usual finger-prick smear
for the microscopes. It was me she sent
on a two-bus journey to the abattoir.

Two weeks into the job and my days so far –
checking Bunsen valves, bottle-brushing
conical flasks, laying out spatulas
on asbestos mats, had not prepared me
for the man in his gore-stained apron,
gloved like a surgeon, that twist
of a smile as he took the empty jam jar,
closed a metal door in my face. No more

than thirty seconds and he handed it back,
slippery-lidded. Unexpected, the thick
warmth carried through glass, the dark
shift of particles inside. A bus caught,
and then another. Cooling in my lap,
that container of pigs' blood, sloshing
beneath its brown paper cover.

Shunkley

It was my mum's friend Sylvia
who gave us the word
which surfaced those rare nights
they went down the Lawnswood Arms

in response to a lurex motif
on a for-best blouse, the dusted-off
lustre of a marcasite brooch:
Jennifer you've got your shunkly on!

And it lingered, the word, to adorn
those first clubbing nights in Leeds –
sequinned dresses shimmering
beneath strobe-lights

before the all-in-black student days
when it revealed itself in a flash
of silver rings, the spark of a nose stud
because it won't be quietened,

this magpie need for a hint of bling –
a jewelled collar, a metallic cuff,
a tinsel halo for Christmas, a diamanté
pendant to lift that little black dress,

my gran on her ninetieth
propped up in a hospice bed,
fingers moving in slow wonder
across the cool facets
of a glass diamond necklace, glittering
hard above the morphine drip.

Fortune Teller Fish

'Place the Fortune Teller Fish in your hand and its movements will indicate your future.'

In those days *Passion* was a total curl-up
willed into being by your teenage self,
a barely-there wafer of cellophane
turning over on your lifeline,
a Christmas-cracker game
where you'd try and wriggle out
of side-lift *Fickle*, back-flip *False*,
the impassive red gleam of the *Dead One*.

A scientist now, you could explain
that whisper-thin strip as hygroscopic –
swelling or receding with the level
of moisture in the skin, a material so light
it shapeshifts on a breath but lay
it on your palm, you'll find yourself wanting
to show you've still got it in you
to raise that *Independent* flag of a tail.

Indian Blue Peacocks For Sale

Just the sight of a feather in a peacock's tail ... makes me sick
– Charles Darwin, 1860

Held on red at the ring road lights
I see the advert scrawled on sawn-off chipboard
a mobile number and price (sixty-five quid)
and I'd quite like to ring and ask if that's for a chick
or a full-grown bird and do peacock breeders
like those who sell puppies   only let them go
to forever homes and wouldn't that be a farm
or even a country estate because didn't I read
that peacocks need space   more than can be found
in sunless back yards and aren't their turquoise
and bronze feathers too insistently luminous

to be trailed over tarmac   displayed against concrete
and how could this small litter-hurling sky
hold their magnificent evolution-defying weight
wouldn't plastic cartons splinter their proud beaks
but just supposing their shimmering throats didn't gag
on the remains of curry sauce and chips   pecked
from the astonished mouths of bins   magine how
musters of them might dust-bathe in gutters   roost
on the cold shoulders of pylons   act out their quivering
deep-blue rituals in the piss-reek alleys of city estates
screech and signal from the bonnets of parked-up cars
and how Darwin would turn away   sickened
by the thought of females having the power to shape
these tails   not at all cock-a-hoop at having
to look again into all those raised eyes

The Dog Who Played With His Shadow

I saw him on the beach, not running
with the other dogs, but bounding back

       and forth, fixated on the moves
       of his darker self, the half-moon quiver

of his tail, the shadow cast on wet sand
that bore the slash marks of his claws.

       Abandoned on the moors, his owner said –
       early life unknown, shed and chain at a guess.

Easy to imagine a shiver of wind,
the resulting stutter of light between slats,

       the dart of a paw, how he worried
       himself half to death, scratched out

the only game he knew on a concrete floor,
a compulsion that fed, grew vast

      on small offerings of sun and shade.
      I remember that expanse of shingle and sky,

those seconds of joyous release before
he pinned himself back to the ground.

Circuit

Seven bars of galvanised steel, ideal for leaning on
to take in a field patched with nettle and docks,
a long view of moorland, copses of sycamore and ash,
and somewhere distant to all this, the motorway.

Horses, fetlock-deep in pale grass, raise heads
when my dog, eight-months and curious,
scrabbles across a slump in the stones.

I call him back, turn at the farmer's laugh.
It's switched off he says *but they don't know that*
and it takes a moment for my vision to snag
on frayed lengths of tape, threaded
through the plastic loops of insulator stakes.

These horses, who've ambled over to stand,
soft-lashed at the gate (though I've nothing to give)
they'll no longer think beyond this field –
its tin bath of water, its buttercups, its circuit
of remembered pain. I leash the dog, walk on,
consider the boundaries of my own life,
which ones might not be live.

Pellets

This is the hour when she thinks of the field,
the unsteady embrace of dry-stone walls,
end-of-summer grasses, whispering
their untidy truths, the tooth-hole ruin

of that barn where she first found the pellets –
dark, neat parcels of feathers and fur,
the pale curve of bone within, each one
packaged up like a gift so she had no choice

but to return every evening, at owl light
and wait for that change in the air, the weight
that comes on silent wings, talons trailing
the tips of the wheat, a half-lifetime ago

and still the bleeding, unseen beneath gold,
the skeletons in her pockets, carried home.

GREG GILBERT

Greg Gilbert is a writer, artist and musician from Southampton and the father of two young girls, ages 5 and 3. In November 2016 he was diagnosed with stage 4 bowel cancer with secondary lung. He is lead singer with the band Delays, who have released 4 albums, and as an artist was a winner of Best in The South of England at the National Open Art Competition and exhibited at the Royal Academy Summer Exhibition. *Love Makes a Mess of Dying* was published as a Laureate's Choice in 2019.

Growing up I was surrounded by storytellers: my family has a rich anecdotal history of supposed 'supernatural' events, which filtered down to me via unquestioning grandparents, aunties, uncles etc – not just ghost stories but mediums, visions, prophecy. All very impressive to a young mind and grist to magical thinking, poetry and drawing. This family folklore and its relationship to place had been the main source of interest for both my writing and artwork, but the cancer diagnosis profoundly changed my creative focus.

I began to write the poems for this collection whilst still in hospital after being diagnosed: diaristic things, observations of life on the ward, trying to understand and confront this illness with as much raw honesty as possible, no matter how uncomfortable. Writing has been an absolute necessity, an attempt to 'own' my situation, and the sequence has been growing ever since.

I had a solo art exhibition at Southampton City Art Gallery in February 2019, based around drawings I made whilst undergoing my first bout of chemotherapy. The publication of the pamphlet coincided with the opening of this exhibition, completing a sense-diary of my experiences as a cancer patient. When I'm not writing, I'm drawing, painting, buying too many books or playing with my two young daughters – this illness has afforded me time to create and be with loved ones, but it is underpinned with great uncertainty.

Love Makes a Mess of Dying

Love makes a mess of dying,
Requires a division of healing
Between what you can allow yourself
And what you can allow others;

It holds you the centre
Of a tolerant universe; such
A simple thing for one, now splintered
Prismatic, unruly.

Love makes a mess of dying,
Rarefies what you've got left and
Draws close those for whom you've been
Essential architecture, each seeking
A totem.

Whatever tricks I tell myself to deaden before dying –
That I'm alone, that alone is the essential state – comes
Undone at the sight of love and I'm afraid, not of dying,
But of leaving a mess for love.

Brother

We overlap, that's the trouble my brother,
Little completions we each bring the other –
Our mother even dressed us the same
Despite our gulf in age – so to separate
Out this catastrophe is an impossibility
Because I know you must wear it
As a weight of support.

On Finding out about the Death of a Schoolmate After His Long Battle with a Brain Tumour

Particular blue arising
From the particular white of day
At evening; old skin thinning
To veins.

Didn't know you'd passed
As I noted the shade
Coming off the windows,
Assumed you'd be forever struggling,
On precipice but still on,
Ahead of our year, taking the
Flak arrows for life. The brave sun
In your face now online
In a hundred tributes and
We all shift a person closer,
The looming unbarred and the
Afterimage of your tears drawing

And evening kept going and became
Something else as you slipped
Off its back without me knowing.

The Sun is God

Each lick of the wind on morning skin,
Branches staggered and awake
Like nerves to every degree
Of the earth's turn; window light
Affords blinding colour – the wince
Of a glorious morning – to eyes
Still precious & sore.

'Intrude' is a word that gives the brain
The shape of it's meaning: like arms
During breaststroke, it has an ease
To its invasion.

Heat intrudes
On cold permanence:
Morning metals, calm and lifeless –
Cars are morning sculptures –
But soon warmth invades,
Evidence of a body,
Evidence we scratch
To retain despite sound proof
Of our being interlopers
In cold permanence.

Brief as dew, there are
Rivers that have never existed,
Oceans that have never sprung
For crossing. We fit where we're
Abandoned and intrusion happens
To everything eventually (right now, needles
Have triumphed over the skin).

Turner's dying words, ' The Sun Is God' – no:
Great cold nothing is the place in which
It all gathers, first and most powerfully.
If there is a God it is utterly blank
Potential and we must make
Peace with peace.

Death Makes a Crown of Love

Death makes a crown of love,
A mantle to take across the threshold
As a sign of accomplished living:
You are loved,
You have loved,
You have lived.

Like Atlantis

It is real, isn't it? This bit of us & the sea?
It could so easily be figment and I wouldn't
Be surprised: I often find myself living
As if the cancer were a fiction, a what-if
Tucked alongside England winning
The World Cup or Yellowstone Park
Erupting.

When I was last here I was so close
To death and didn't know it but photos
From that day preserve our complete denial
(One small wave could've snapped me,
My arms around the kids less than sand), now
A barely recognised season I feel
I once felt. But here we are again, briefly
Escaped & thicker set: the kissing coast
Adored by breakers that've rolled
From God knows where to land at our bare feet –
I don't remember the last time we were alone
With the sea and yet I can't say the thing I need to say:

"I don't want to die".

You can't give me what I need in return
And it would only make you feel helpless,
That's the selfish truth, and with our view
Set upon the sliding vastness it seems

A shame to shrink it to my life span.
Let's set this illness upon it
With our hurt: 18 months bruised
By 'living with it, not dying from it',
Only now knowing what that actually means:

Not content to chew my gut it gnawed us
Livid, it poisoned us, not until enemies but
Strangers.

Let's picture it all now adrift on the glassy jade
and beg: smash it like Atlantis, will you?

A ceremony of care: we have no stone
Effigy but we do have the sea, the world's
Water thrown at us, and it's not hard
To imagine every ripple ever cast still living
Inside it, every voice lost upon it
Still reverberating below science,
Like some great warehouse of moment. Take
The prognosis, take the anguish, the comforting
Words, the arguments and desperation
And stash them deep and make them other
Whilst we reify our place, here, amongst
The living.

It is real, isn't it? This bit of us & the sea?
This, here, could be just three brushstrokes:
Sand, teal & cut cyanide.

Tree Envy (The Field Again)

Look at me in this field again,
You'd never guess there was a sky:
All suggestion and receding, the sun
Made peach by river mist,
The bare trees edgeless
And tissue-rent, I more so and fitting.

The ideation has been growing,
Not a plan you understand – I reassure
My therapist there are no plans –
But thoughts are a damp towel over
A chip-pan-fire, they suffocate
The spitting fat, but not the act –
I'm a coward and besides, love.

Not annihilation then, but I envy
The trees their shrouded morning
Where you wouldn't know them unless
You were at their feet. These limits
Make a realm in which I've shed so much –
The lip spit of kisses, the grease
Of burnt tyres and stolen engines.

At least one layer of this paling field
Is me and I watch me go without dying,
A forecast to behold and live: as the birds,
Bodiless, chorus this devour,
Its threshold – ash, fir and cow-parsley –
Slipping to milk with my eyes just
Articles in space.

Overheard Couple in a Café / Café Life as Distraction

If I sit back, the sun misses me
And hits the couple next to me
Locked in doing life what you want –
Repeated, do what you want – and 'Cold Sweat'
Grinds against the window. The sun becomes
A molten finger through the window,
The couple next to me mention New York,
Vegas – change of faces; this is a moment
This a lever of life, why not if you have the talent
And skills – a dog-leg of being taking place
Whilst I sit back and let the sun miss me;
Living through dog-leg with hands over eyes –
It's a 'Family Affair' now no one can
Ever make you feel bad, the woman
Says little the man pours out such giving.
Thank you.

KEITH HUTSON

Keith Hutson has written for Coronation Street and for many well-known comedians. He is also a published playwright. His poetry features in journals including *The North*, *The Rialto*, *Stand*, *Magma*, *Agenda*, *The Manhattan Review*, and *Poetry Salzburg Review* where he is now on the editorial board. His debut pamphlet, *Routines*, was published in 2016 by Poetry Salzburg. Keith has an MA (Poetry) from Manchester Metropolitan University. He delivers poetry and performance workshops for the Square Chapel Theatre and Children And The Arts. Keith's debut full collection, *Baldwin's Catholic Geese*, is published in 2019 by Bloodaxe. *Troupers* was published as a Laureate's Choice in 2018.

When I was twenty, I bought a copy of The New Oxford Book Of Light Verse, *edited by Kingsley Amis. As someone who had failed the (then very basic) police entrance exam, not to mention CSE Maths, I was impressed by the word 'Oxford'. The book not only showed me that 'light verse' can be delightfully dark, but it also treated me to several very funny limericks and music hall-type monologues. I had been brought up to appreciate light entertainment on stage and TV, which led, later in life, to writing for comedians, so this book was a perfect introduction to, perhaps not the higher, but the different, art of poetry.*

When I finished the book, I was hooked, addicted, to rhyme, regular rhythm, profundity sugar-coated with glibness, sparkling narrative, clarity, and I still am. Rib-tickling but quality poetry that is more than the sum of its parts, deserves to be taken seriously. Humour illuminates truth.

I do, however, like to tell myself my reading has broadened and deepened over the years, but my default mode remains poets who can make me smile, appropriately or not, whilst smuggling in some thoroughgoing thoughts, and accomplishing this, in the main, through work that respects, pushes, and plays with, traditional form.

Writing about the extraordinary, hard, often short, lives of music hall and Variety artistes is, for me, a labour of love.

Revival

Like the funniest of men, he had that look:
bad health crossed with indestructibility.
Fans would slap and cuddle him.

It takes a certain type of body to appear,
night after night, as if a gang's manhandled
it into a dinner suit; face folded
like a heart attack was homing in.

It was. But he'd soaked several up already;
recovered with a crack:
Treading boards is my best exercise!

After the last, wrapped in an overcoat
on Blackpool prom, he'd seemed robust enough,
just pale. And people like him, whose fathers

died in harness, whose mothers bore silent,
determined lives, they never bow out barely used.
One way or another they sweat buckets,
under stress, and make that state hilarious.

That's why we wet ourselves when they collapse
at the Palladium. And why it's only right
to raise another smile, to bring them back.

Straight Man

You think you could be me, don't you?
The nobody who's only there to prop
the patter up. The one who, deadpan,
asks the obvious to set the silly answers free.

You think you could be me but better.
Make more of an effort. Be a super-feed.
Do so much more than look disdainful.

Try it, then. Try not to smile.
Be subliminal lit by a bank of lights.
Try keeping control, reining in an idiot;
forcing the pace so he can fly.

Try to pitch a put-down perfectly
and, backstage, be the chipper one who copes
with nerves, neurosis. Do the admin too.

Try this for size: the difference between us,
you and me, is I *pretend* I'm dull.
And that barrel of laughs who acts
like he should be locked up –
he is. Try being the key.

Hostess Trolley

Often employed in Alan Ayckbourn plays,
this one, as soon as it was wheeled on stage,
loaded with nibbles, drinkie-poos, began
to concertina. Which it would, when some
fool hadn't locked the catch. Geoffrey, who no
amount of pancake could remould into
a suave young architect, couldn't let go
of it throughout the second act. Where he
went, it went, and the bending made his tight
suit trousers look half-mast. Then his back seized.
During the interval, we tried some holds
and tugs that made it worse. He's still not right,
we've heard: no one from our lot ever sees
him, now he's cast so well for playing bowls.

Hylda

i.m. Hylda Baker 1909-1986

Nine was the age the likes of her learnt
how to lip-read at the mill;
to flap their silent mouths in turn.

But Hylda found her voice inside this act,
talent that kept her in pink gins for years:
a *popular comedienne*, bottom of the bill.

Funny, then, to be described by Delfont
as an overnight success, *proprietress*
of Pledge's Pickle Factory on ITV.

They said that show went to her head.
Deaf to them, she changed her tipple to a lot
of crème de menthe, bought a bungalow

in Cleveleys, quilted bedroom floor to ceiling,
cocktail bar an opera box, doorbell
singing *Come Back To Sorrento*

as she warned reporters,
Don't be dazzled by the décor –
it's contemporary.

Barred from playing panto dame,
she made her men wear dresses, let them stay
on the condition they were dumb.
Her harem swelled, and neighbours,
outraged yet refined, presented a petition:
Please leave. Thank you.

This prompted the flagpole with
You haven't had the pleasure of me yet
flown every day and twice for matinees.

Spandex at seventy, that bump-and grind
with Arthur Mullard on Top Of The Pops,
and then she died, demented,

utterly alone – unmourned
by impresarios and sisterhoods alike.
Nine was the number at her funeral.

Glasgow Empire

Yes, it was here the gang show audience
slow-handclapped that girl guide
with laryngitis;

the Beverley Sisters flitted on
then promptly darted off again
to cries of *Christ, there's three of 'em!*

Where else would Eartha Kitt
be forced back out, Ken Dodd
having cut his act in half?

After Des O'Connor fainted
from derision, dragged to safety,
seventy ice creams were counted on his suit.
Even when empty, anger
occupied this auditorium. It bloomed,
silent and black: a storm building to break

above row upon row of folded seats,
all rigid as a nervous herd
before it bolts.

Accept No Imitations

i.m. J D Plummer 1846-1901

Do your colleagues call you a control freak?
Fuck 'em. Abandoned on the first night
by his cast, J D played every character
himself: Dick Turpin, victims, innkeeper
and black-eyed daughter Bess, Dick's worn-out horse,
also called Bess, and black (this did cause
confusion), Tom the Ostler who betrayed them,
weeping Widow Shelley, Tyburn hangman,

and it ran for fifteen months, through Glossop,
Leeds and York, till he collapsed banging two
coconuts together at a gallop,
then went bankrupt, then insane. Worth it, though,
to show incompetents what can be done
by one who stands, delivers, falls, alone.

Clever Bugger

i.m. Bob Monkhouse 1928-2003

Why did we laugh, but never love you, Bob?
Some claimed you came across as insincere.
So what? You were a comic, not the pope.
Perhaps that calculated gulp before
each punchline, patter too precision-made,
anecdotes too pleased with one another,
plus your business acumen and tan, said
Clever Bugger never *National Treasure*

till, with weeks to live, bloated and slow from
drugs, you begged all men, on *Parkinson*,
to take a prostate test. Too late for you,
but what a warm performance, funny too –
it won us critics over there and then:
smart move, Bob, dying *such a decent man.*

Lament

i.m. Sing Something Simple 1959-2001

Sunday afternoons gave up the ghost
to this: a lone accordion
held little comfort as the theme tune
faded into half an hour of shadow,
cast across the country
by the Light Programme.

It came to rival *Songs of Praise*
for sudden deaths:
the tender preface could have been
Why not lie back
and ponder ways to end
it all without alarming others.

At eight I joined a boxing club
that met when it was on the radiogram.
An expert might conjecture
I preferred a fat lip to Cliff Adams
and his choir, for over forty years
kept artificially alive:

that's ten prime ministers,
all looking grim. The folk who tuned in
first, from choice, are falling now.
But they were tough – took any measure
of *make-do* thrown at them,
could survive on airwaves if required.

FAITH LAWRENCE

Faith Lawrence lives in Manchester and makes radio programmes exploring language and poetry for the BBC. She wrote about the art of listening for her Creative Writing PhD at the University of St Andrews, and is compiling a glossary of 'listening' words (whilst keeping an ear out for her young son, who is usually quite easy to hear). Her poems have been published in *Poetry Review* and *The Interpreter's House*. *Sleeping Through* was published as a Laureate's Choice in 2019.

One of the poems in this selection came out of a favourite memory: paddling in a lido on a sunny day, when I was about six, with a packet of Monster Munch in my hands (pickled onion flavour). In the poem the lido is not just a lido, but a vision of the afterlife. I like the way a poem can take something slight, and make it a portal for something else.

Some poets have started to talk about 'listening' for their poems, and I'm interested in what that means. Kathleen Jamie has talked about 'listening with attention ... not just with the ear' – listening to language, but also listening as a metaphor for a particular kind of attention. It's the bits of my poems that feel heard, rather than written, that seem to work.

Around the same time as that lido experience, I don't know why, but I decided to learn a poem by heart. We had a poetry anthology at home – Robert Louis Stevenson's A Child's Garden of Verses, *but only this poem looked manageable: 'The world is so full of a number of things / I'm sure we should all be as happy as kings'. It's a strange, terse little thing, but I remember the pleasure of the full rhyme, and the lovely plenitude of it: ('so full of a number of things'). I don't think it's because of Stevenson, but I still find myself wanting to read and write small poems I can hold in my head – but which might have it in them to reach beyond the hearing of the poet or even the poem.*

It's also deeply satisfying, when you're in the middle of all the noise, chat, and consuming flow of mothering a small child, to try and rescue a moment from that flow, something that would otherwise be lost, and to let the white space on a page gently amplify it. A lot of the work I admire, (by George Herbert, Kathleen Jamie, Don Paterson, Sharon Olds, W S Graham) seems to have this generous listening space around it.

Grace

Of the visitors
that spring

I remember
the queen bee

levitating her heavy
body through

an open window
her balance

in resistance,
her hovering

at the very edge
of probability

Delivery

Baby, you took your time;
nothing else was in the world
until you found that ring
of bone, and clever as a key
you turned, slipped right
through and unlocked me.

Sleeping Through

He wakes, reaches
for my hand and says
'it's very morning',
which is true.
The sky is lanolin,
dressed for business
as he kisses me
and smiles with that
rough new
tenderness of his –
then it's time to get up,
time for breakfast,
and this is why
I write no poems –
my boy singing
to his tiny trains,
a day with no interstices,
beautiful as usual.

Close

Now evening comes
the way you slow
down a swing –

the way you hold
your child to the seat
to steady them.

Afterlife

Heaven is a lido on the coast
where the dead are playing catch
in swimming costumes
and flowery bathing caps
everyone's losing their teeth
but they seem to be loving it.

Look at the lunches they bring:
ham sandwiches and crisps,
fruit and sponge cake for afters.
Hear them laughing on the sand,
the waves dashing their rumours
as they glide beneath the water.

Ritual

When I was locked out last night
the house was all lit up, glowing
like a church on Christmas Eve –
I saw men and women in the hallway
walking in silence, trailing
long grey robes up the staircase
and I knew they were heading
for the room where you were sleeping.
They seemed to be expecting
a birth or a death; but of that
I cannot tell you anything.

Gift

Dark at five. The gift of winter
is to limit us, to make morning
in an hour, the day in miniature.

RACHEL MCCARTHY

Rachel McCarthy's poems have been broadcast on BBC Radio and Sky TV – the latter as a commission for Anthony Gormley's 'Fourth Plinth' project – and some appeared in their early form in print, most notably in *Shearsman Magazine*. *Element* was published as a Laureate's Choice in 2015.

I write exclusively at home in Exeter, in the main bedroom of my apartment, which I converted into a study. I've never been the type to go and sit scribbling in a café – it's too distracting. To me poetry requires so much concentration, not just when the pen hits the page, but maybe as much as days or weeks before. Trying to write next to a milk-frothing machine makes that impossible. I mostly write at night, having a strict rule of being in my study by 8pm at the very latest. This allows me a break between work and writing, but not so long that I'm too tired to concentrate. I use the weekend days to edit, as then I am clear-headed. I've found that editing directly after writing (or even worse – during) means you don't see the trees for the wood. Outside of writing my job takes up most of my time. I'm a senior scientist at the Met Office, specialising in the impacts of climate change and science communication.

Element has been almost five years in the making. I've written a few poems outside of it, but it has been the main focus since I moved to Devon in 2008. I've written essays elsewhere – as a scientist having a framework to hang my theories (poems in this case) from has been helpful. This gave me an initial structure to explore poetry within. Research into each of the elements came next. I studied outside my work hours, not just chemistry but history too, the classics, to expand my knowledge base, to build up to the point I could dive off of and into the poem. I learnt to be patient. You have to let knowledge and ideas ferment. Research doesn't generate poems, but it can enable them. The driving forces of any poem are emotion, rhythm and sound.

28
Ni
nickel

Memorial at Norilsk

We're close
the pines thinning out and our road a slew
steering us into the wide, blank stare of the Steppes.

The sky stops its colour.
The storm from the East purges – whiteout
as though the Earth herself gulped those men down

gulag, gulag, gulag, gulag, gulag.

In Tura they told us come spring
bones of fingers and toes
knuckle their way up like snowdrops.

I'm conspicuous but unwatched,
anonymous in this terrible landscape.
I've never slaved a day in my life, not like that,

not with such yearning, such muttered song,
so here are the meagre flowers,
the bend to one knee

precipitating the howl
toward speech, each petal
blazing.

Pellestrina

We could make it here: two buses and a boat away from civilisation
on this sickle of sand, this searing heaven,
all sky, sky and the tide blending, cerulean,
become zenithed, heightened.
I could survive on sun and sleep,
grow thin and strong, run clean
as long as you stand there – where my mind holds you
pointing out what I'd otherwise miss:
a crab shuttling for cover,
a cormorant's needle-dive into the swell,
the moon-round of a jellyfish,
its bell pulsating with light.

Riddle

I'm a beginning born from an end:
stars die bearing me.
My youth cries
fire, anvil, hammer.
I kill but can't be blamed.
Middle-aged, I'm the highest honour
of fallen empires –
for Russia they hung me by a red silk ribbon.
In the end though Wales is my lodestone,
those purpose-built towns
where Thatcher had it in for me –
my death the derivation of irony.

Abandoned Airfield at Dunkeswell

The height of summer. I thread my shadow
along the runway's vein of moss.
Nothing remains to mark the point
from which to look down
the length of sun-soft strip
that speeds back to this:
the hangar's simple machines of history,
the pop-rivet gun and punch clock,
the workbench morse-code of chisel and nail.

Pray for the fathers who took flight
that they lifted themselves away gently
but also for those housed in echoing halls
returning year after year
like swallows, to build.

Postcard of a Break-Up Written at
Edinburgh Castle

To tell you about the weather
I should first explain how the Sun –
sluggish with the weight of winter –
rolls back the haar.
To compare the city's slow reveal
to a bride lifting her veil,
although accurate,
misleads.

Dear John,
I'm sorry I didn't write a letter
but in short see reverse
for a picture of Mons Meg
the most powerful cannon ever built
which turned out to be a damp squib.

The Visitation

Night rolls out its road.
We speed along hedged by dark forest dark sea,
ink-coarse, formless but impenetrable,
dumbfounded the Moon slips away to recover herself
leaving our headlights the sole source of light,
zoetropes repeating a scope of bramble and fern
until a stag – caught mid-step on the bank –
a momentary megalith of antler and flank.

You didn't see him, held, hallucinatory
and the visitation over so quickly
I couldn't be sure, but I felt a poverty
as though some great knowledge passed me.
What'll become of us – the Moon's corollary –
hurtling, speechless.
How a sharp turn of the wheel
could save or discard us.

The Moon to the Sun Approaching Eclipse

Each night brings you closer; I wait, tethered
to the sea, reflect on my life ploughing
furrows in water, my litany of wrecks.
I'm an old penny – my body dull but its vow
still peaks wave-bright – like you, I long to be spent;
flare the way a match flares down to its heart
submit to the inevitable length
of our stately practiced arc.

Yet though you and I know the other lonely,
we'll only bring the Earth to a brief stop,

our pas de deux a dance of two solos
each half a gift of our oppositeness:

me a flitter of warmth and light, alive,
you spinning dumbly through the night.

Ghost Shark

Millions of years on
Megalodon swims its half ghost
through the ether of museum-space
part-shark part-reconstructed cartilage
top-jaw hoisted for a pig-eyed profile
made an example of.

But who's to say unequivocally
that at this exact moment she's not
holed-up in the wreck of an old war
nursing in the cold vault of our history
or charnel-mouthed over its huddled bodies
who's to say there's no glint in her dead eyes.

After all where better to see-out extinction
than from beyond the last glimmer of sunlight
where her movements sound like whispers
in our deep water soundings.
Who's to say she isn't just beyond our reach
Who's to say she shouldn't stay that way.

MARK PAJAK

Mark Pajak's work has appeared in *The London Review of Books*, *Poetry London*, *The North*, *The Rialto* and *Magma*. He has been commended in the National Poetry Competition, awarded first place in The Bridport Prize and has also received a Northern Writers' Award, an Eric Gregory Award and an UNESCO international writing residency. *Spitting Distance* was published as a Laureate's Choice in 2016.

At school, learning difficulties meant my literacy was poor and so I struggled. But my mum would tell me about Stephen Wiltshire, the artist who grew up with autism and didn't speak until he was seven. It was this – combined with my dad reading Burns to me (where patterns of sound unlocked words in a way that prose couldn't) – which woke in me that first deep want to be a writer. That is what got me started. However, now it is the work of other poets that sustains me.

When I'm out running and there's a vapour trail overhead, I remember the line 'a skater's track / across the icy sky' *and then back home I reread Robertson. Drizzle past my train window becomes* 'stacks of rain … collapsing sideways' *and I put my earphones in, listen to MP3s of Armitage. Walking home one autumn, I noticed the flickering in a gusted tree and this triggers one of Alice Oswald's stanzas:*

> *Like leaves*
> *Sometimes they light their green flames*
> *And are fed by the earth*
> *And sometimes it snuffs them out*

The strength of these images (and others like them) have laced themselves into my perception of the world, their triggers hidden everywhere. Their exactness or sound texture or inventiveness fuel my imagination and compel me to write.

After Closing Time
for Joe

We head to the edge of town,
to the black river and old stone bridge.

Two boys full of vodka,
tipping side to side like flames.

And for a laugh, we climb
the railing and hang from our arms.

Below in the deep, two boys
peer up at us over their feet.

Like drops of water
we are gathering ourselves to fall.

One of us says, *You go first,*
and we echo this back and forth.

We are here for a very long time.
Years in fact. I marry. Divorce.

You skip all that, become a father.
We see less and less of each other.

Now we are what the world
considers 'men'. Which is to say

we've learnt that falling is inevitable.
Yet here we are still, side by side,

two boys way past closing time,
holding on until the other lets go.

Brood

... and in their glance was permanence
– John Berger

At sixteen, I did a day's work
on an egg farm.
A tin shed the size of a hangar.

Inside its oven dark
two thousand stacked cages,
engines of clatter and squawk.

My job, to pass a torch
through the bars for the dead hens
and pack them tight into a bin bag.

All the time my mind chanting:
there's only one hen. Just one
ruined hen repeated over and over.

In this way I soothed the sight
of all that caged battery,
their feathers stripped to stems,

their patches of scrotum skin,
their bodies held
in the dead hands of their wings.

But what kept me awake
that hot night in my box room,
as I listened to the brook outside

chew on its stones and the fox's
human scream, was how
those thousand-thousand birds

had watched me. And really
it was me repeated over and over,
set in the amber of their eyes.

Me, the frightened boy in jeans
stiff with chicken shit, carrying
a bin bag full of small movement.

A foot that opened. An eyelid
that unshelled its blind nut.
A beak mouthing a word.

My Dead Grandmother

Here is a rope-swing; its blue plait slung
from a branch. Sat there on its knot,
bare feet planted on the riverbank, is Gran.

Stood beside her, my dad watches the river
– its spate frayed white on small rocks –
his eyes black pebbles under thick glasses.

But Gran's eyes are full of distance, watching
nothing. Her gown breathes-in the breeze,
and her hospice reek, that chemical rot,

meets my father's face thick as damp cloth.
But he says nothing. Just lets the river whisper
its shush of water. Then he gives his *wee mammy*

a push. The swing halves the air like paper.
And as she moves away, her weight
just enough to crack the rope's long spine,

my dad, left behind on the riverbank,
is both the man watching the swing go
and the boy aching for the swing back.

Spitting Distance

Near Edale, I find a live rifle shell
like a gold seed in the earth.

So I load it into my mouth
and go on walking, the sun

breathing down my neck,
the head of Mam Tor rising

and the path falling like a braid.
So this is what it's like to be a gun;

copper bleeding on the gums,
the domino click in the teeth.

At the blue summit, I look down
with my new perspective

on the warped floor of Derbyshire,
to where a village pools in a valley

and a chimney hangs from the sky
on a white string. And I watch

with hunger the red dot of a car
stop at a crossroads. I suck hard

on the blunt bud, drawing out
its deeper flavour of powder,

smoke down the barrel
of my throat. Then it hits me

that there's another side to this.
And I lay in the warm heather.

A body with a bullet
in its head staring at this sky.

Its clouds blown open.
Its sudden night.

Thin

Collie dog
locked
in a shed
in Toxteth.
Dead.
We shoved
the door in
found him
thin.
A bin bag
of cutlery,
a cider pint
stink. Flies
in the spoons
of his eye sockets.
Scraps of fur
crumbed
with blood.
Empty shelves
of ribs
and the pear stalk
of his penis.
Dead. Until
I touched him
and he whined
like a knife
scraping a plate.
Rattled the rinds
of his tail.

Cat on the Tracks

He wore the night in his fur, sat on a rung
between the rails, tail wisping like smoke

as a distant train split the air along its seam.
Its coming headlight laid down track

and placed an opal into each black seed
of the cat's eyes, every blink slow as an eclipse.

Soon the white light pinned him, the only drop
of night left as vibration turned the rails to mercury.

But there was no give in the cat, no flex anywhere
but his tail. And for a moment their roles reversed,

as though it were the train facing the inevitable cat,
the end of the line. The world lit up like a page

and the train a sentence before the full-stop.

Dear Neighbour in the Flat Above

last night I mistook you for falling snow.
In bed I heard my ceiling purr as if
collecting your weight, as though you settled
up there in perfect layers. Then I dreamt
your flat really did fill with soft powder;
an empty table took on a white cloth,
a wood floor heaped to a shag carpet,
a bed beneath a growing feathered quilt.

But when the ceiling started to shiver
I woke. Your noise grown heavy. And then I
realised that there were two of you up there,

making heat. Not grains of snow gathering
on your skins but rain. And my room felt cold.
Its pale bulb flickered. Plaster drifted down.

Camping on Arran, 1992

Dad, you had shared with me your sleeping bag.
And we lay like hands held in one pocket.
When the dark flickered and a pause before

thunder; a sound like the sky waking.
And waking with it, I trembled; trapped,
a boy in a storm, in this tight space

ripe with your sleeping man's body.
But when the canvas flared again
white with a hem of shadow grass,

you were awake and counting
down the seconds to thunder.
And I, listening, was struck still.

As each count became less
– the storm brighter, louder –
I could feel a closeness

like breath in the air.
And I fell asleep
as rain would fall; soft,

then in a rush.
You counting us
into the eye.

WAYNE PRICE

Wayne Price was born in South Wales but has lived and worked in Scotland since 1987, teaching at the University of Aberdeen. His short stories and poems have been widely published and won many awards. His debut story collection, *Furnace* (Freight, 2012), was shortlisted for the Saltire Scottish First Book of the Year and long-listed for the Frank O'Connor Award. His first novel, *Mercy Seat*, was published in February 2015. He was a finalist in the Manchester Poetry Competition in both 2013 and 2014. *Fossil Record* was published as a Laureate's Choice in 2015.

Growing up in the Welsh valleys during the Thatcher years I had a fairly limited sense of what poetry was, and what it might be for. My family was working class but we always had books in the house – mainly Reader's Digest editions, but also a Palgrave's, a selection from the Romantics and, by some happy chance, the Helen Gardner Oxford Book of English Verse. Through those, and the odd poem we studied at school, I become fascinated by reading and writing poetry in my early teens. At that stage my sense of what a 'modern' kind of poetry might sound like was almost wholly shaped by Yeats, Eliot and Dylan Thomas, and the more I came to realise that my own raw materials were completely unsuited to their voices and methods, the more I despaired of ever finding an honest and unpretentious voice of my own. Basically, my poetry reading was two generations out of date, and it didn't help that my worldview at the time was even more anachronistic: cobbled together from incongruous chunks of Romanticism, strict chapel Calvinism and Marxism. I could see the Beats and the Mersey poets waving in the smoky distance, but I had too much nineteenth century baggage on my back to do anything more than wave enviously back.

Just as I reached this crisis of confidence I started university and discovered the stories of Raymond Carver and Bobbie Ann Mason. Their understated, luminous grittiness seemed, with the force of a revelation, exactly the solution I was looking for. In a fit of adolescent zeal I threw out all my poems and notebooks and started completely afresh as a writer, in prose. It took me over twenty years to start talking in poetry again after that mistake, but I'm not completely sorry. I've learned that the poetry I write is simply what I can't do in prose, and vice-versa – I think that's a useful discipline, and how it should be.

Nightfishing

Hand and mind are fishing the river after dark
for the slow, heavy old ones that rise at night.

The white feathers on the hook are spread
like wings on a moth. Mind watches them travel down

the bright lane the moon makes. A white moon and the white bait.
The line in hand grows heavy with the river's black weight.

Or it is an indoor scene: the moon's fluorescent silver on the stream
is the night light over beds in the emergency room.

In the deepest pools the trout, heavy as sacks of sand,
are swaying in their gravel bowls, between the big stones.

Their bodies shape their homes. They have fattened
on smaller shapes that were images of their own.

Hand and mind are fishing for a nest of forms.
Like an egg in a nest of clouds, the moon.

The bait is a moth that has battened on the window pane.
As mind stares out, it stares in. Like chains the hooks and lines

of drugs and salt and blood to hands. Mind is fishing between
the banks of beds. Like moonlight, one light always on.

Witness

I've followed the older boys stealing milk
from doorsteps at dawn, after long pale nights
in summer spent camping on the rugby ground.
When they took them from my own front door
I never complained. And I watched them hang
a screaming friend of mine by his ankles from
the quarry cliff, then watched him hoisted back again.

I've stood and watched as Benny Griffiths took
a kicking that nearly killed him, outside
the Workingmen's Hall. He curled inwards like a snail
until the toes of those big boots had picked
his skinny body loose like string; I watched
by the cenotaph, late, in the rain. Years
I've watched myself watching. These and other things.

Crows, Seaton Park

The green of afternoon
is spooling backwards to grey. Flats
of water on the football pitch
mirror like tin.

I have counted
twenty-nine crows on the playing field,
upright, silent, discretely spaced,
professionally still.
They have clasped
their wings behind their backs
like undertakers' hands.

What are they waiting for?
They ignore the faint sounds
of the last of the children

dropping to their feet
from the climbing frames; the voices
of mothers pushing prams.

Finally, like a man
remembering the time, one
flaps toward the woods
and disappears.
All around
a heaviness has landed,
like a great, inexplicable craft,
its landing gear
acres wide, sinking
through the evening air
onto flooded ground,
onto slides and benches, onto creaking,
stiff-chained swings;
the crows taking
flight at first, then settling, incurious,
on its cooling wings.

Hey Water

Ten years now you've been gone. This morning, a boy
of three or four, loud and brassy as a school bell,
raced round the back of this farmhouse hotel
and saw the bright zinc pipe that bleeds water
from the heavy hill and splashes it to an open drain.

I was back there to smoke a cigarette. I nodded
and said hello but it was only the clatter of falling
water he listened to. He froze and watched it flare in the sun.
Hey water! Where you going? he yelled, then spun away
at once of course, having no interest in the answer.

Surfers, Carrowmore Strand

Lowry might have painted these
simple lives in the foam; approximate
black stick-figures, flocked as if for company
but absorbedly separate and alone.

Their brief paths cross over crumbling ruins.
Most lie flat, can barely evolve
to crouch or kneel, slide open-mouthed, face-on
into a simmer that is nobody's

land, that shifts its million territories
moment by moment under them.
The sea is too big for some; they tire
and stagger ashore, one by one. Others

grow younger, flinging themselves sideways
as they fall, as if blasted out of the water.
They are always choosing the wrong wave,
but simply choose another; are so content

to get so little right. They are disappearing
in a white moment that comes
again and again. They are practicing
abandoning everything, everyone.

Dead Hawk, the Anglican
Churchyard, Tangier

It is lighter at the tips
of my fingers than
the snap-out balsa planes
I made as a boy

and launched from
my bedroom window
on afternoons of Welsh rain
to a bare strip of garden.

Days of sun and wind
have whittled it clean
to stiff pinion
feathers and bone.

Cats stalk the desiccated
grasses between
the graves, but none of them
have dismantled it;

it has only been
troubled from within,
and all the hidden turmoil
that churned there is done.
The ebony crescent
of its beak is still
precise and fine. I can
see clean through

the empty house
of the skull,
like the quality
of a memory

the mind has refined,
to the gardener
with his combing rake,
who like the cats

has let it lie,
and to the dusty green
leaves above, and the
clean blue sky.

Not the Place but How the Place Was Found

Travelling lost is one way to get there
(not the place but how the place was found);
falling and lying all night is another.
The rooms that filled with snow, the quick black river
I fished and followed underground;
drowned bells in the loch at the heart of the moor.

Two beetles I poured from a graveside jar
were rowing to get there, round and round.
I know this road but not the places. Where your
house should stand is a foreign town.
Travelling lost is one way to get here.
Not the place but how the place was found.

Fossil Record

Wind was stammering at the windows all night.
If I slept at all it was a half-sleep
filled with thoughts that halved into dreams
and back again. The first cells divided
identically, for millions of years.
Millions of years before difference began.

Slow learning life. Slower than stone. I would
like a sleep as deep as those first fractal
animals, colourless, rooted in the dark
of empty oceans, carbon-paper thin.

Everything in the wind says give me time,
I can change: minerals in the rocks and streams;
proteins in warm seas; memories; children
who will remind us they never asked to be born.

YVONNE REDDICK

Yvonne Reddick's pamphlet *Translating Mountains* (Seren, 2017) won the *Mslexia* Magazine Pamphlet competition and was selected as a favourite pamphlet of the year in the *TLS*. Her work appears in *PN Review*, *Poetry Ireland Review*, *Stand* and *The North*. She has won a Northern Writer's Award, the Poetry Society's Peggy Poole Award, a commendation in the 2018 National Poetry Competition and a Creative Futures Literary Award. In 2017 she was a Hawthornden Fellow and a Jerwood/Arvon mentee. She is an associate board member of *Magma* magazine and the author of *Ted Hughes: Environmentalist and Ecopoet*. *Spikenard* was published as a Laureate's Choice in 2019.

I started writing when I borrowed my dad's battered old school copy of The New Poetry. *It was 1999, the pages of the anthology were yellowed with age, and the poems weren't especially new – but they were a revelation to me. I then read English at Cambridge and received my PhD from the University of Warwick.*

I am especially interested in how poetry engages with environmental issues. I'm currently writing a book about poetic responses to local and global environmental problems – which involves reading Ted Hughes's terrible handwriting and Seamus Heaney's postcards to him.

Spikenard *began its life during a Hawthornden Fellowship. The title poem started out as a response to John Burnside's poem of obsessive jealousy, 'Moon Going Down,' but with the gender roles changed. When I asked for a second opinion about my draft from other poets, someone I respect told me to cut the details of the lovers' lives, bodies and actions and go straight for the scent of the perfume. I'm pleased that I did.*

Desire Path

Once, we thought we'd find a route around the borders
and feel the bounds dissolve, like sutures in a wound.
So my hands roved the path of your spine, and my lowland mouth
spoke your Highlander surname – tried it on like a ring.
I'd flash you the glance you called *that French look*
as you followed the curve of my back, the contours of my flank,
then I slid my Genevan tongue in your ear: *Je t'aime, moi non plus,*
as if I'd become two speakers who split and merged

as tides braid, then loose, the waters of the Channel.
And my fingers with the quickness of a Hann violinist
read your palms, the image of your grandfather's –
the one who'd call the foals in his Galway brogue.
Oh, I could ride you for miles in one night, unbitted,
without straying an inch from your bed.

Firesetter

You left me a two-word note. Lying
under our bed was your forgotten lighter.
I ran to the forest and held its flame to a fir-cone –

the resiny scales hissed like a Molotov cocktail.
I hurled it over your deer fence into
the spruces where we once heard nightjars.

Three months of drought; those trees were jackstraws.
A flicker in the tinder, bird-call panic.
The easterly sighed on the flames as I walked away.

I pictured your garden: a sheaf of flaming letters
where the paper birch once stood.
The oaks, hands of bone with a furnace backdrop.

Two days in, my brushfire had swallowed fifty hectares.
Sirens through the heat-haze,
villagers were silhouettes with hose reels.

Peat earth: fire skulked underground at a smoulder.
Wheat burned from the root up.
On the third day, a rain of soot. The school stood empty.

Nine days on, fire-crews drained the lake,
the village abandoned under a haze.
The ninth night – I found the staircase

leading to air, the bedroom blasted open,
the ribs and roof-tree smoking.
You stepped from the door's charred gape.

In Amber

They've been coupled fifty million years:
the pair of midges trapped in Baltic amber.
Antennae of the male like thistledown fronds,
the female's wedding-veil wings, her body umber.

She sipped the blood of mousebirds and dawn horses,
he flew to her wingbeats' call. Landing on timber,
they mated – facing opposite ways, yet tender –
now trapped in the pine-tree's tears, liquid embers.

Voyeur with a lens, I spy on what's left of their lust.
The resin clasps three bubbles of fossil air:
if I broke them, I could breathe the past.
So why did you give me their long-spent affair

in this gem last May, but leave in December?
I dig out your number – almost type, '*Do you remember?*'

The Bait

With strangling snare, or windowy net – John Donne

You were two years gone. I swallowed the hook of his smile.
He poured me wine, dark as a wound; wouldn't drink,
but coiled a tattooed arm around my waist.
He said he'd sear a quail's breast for me.

I poured him wine, dark as a wound; wouldn't drink.
When he asked to come to my place, I told him *no*.
He said he'd sear a quail's breast for me –
he'd turn the flame up high, it would take a few minutes.

When he came to my place, I told him *no*,
but he had to show me his cooking – I'd be impressed.
He'd turn the flame up high: it would take a few hours.
He caught my wrist. His grip was a snare,

he had to show me his cock – I'd be impressed –
it felt like a bolt-gun, pressing the base of my spine.
He pinioned my arm, his grip was a snare
and my no was the carved-out tongue of a doe.

It felt like a bolt-gun at the base of my spine –
I wrenched free, burst through the door,
my no the carved-out tongue of a doe.
Damn you, long-gone lover, for not breaking his jaw.

I wrenched free, burst through the door –
fuck these numb fists for not breaking his jaw.
My brother: 'You wore jeans – what did you expect?'
My mother: 'You invited him in – what did you expect?'

You were two years gone; I swallowed the hook of his smile
when he coiled a tattooed arm around my waist.
I still feel hands tighten like snares in my sleep.
Damn these numb fists. My gun by the bolted door.

Muirburn

My father weighed a little less than at birth.
I carried him in both hands to the pines
as October brought the burning season.
When I unscrewed the urn, bone-chaff and grit
streamed out, with their gunpowder smell.
      I remembered the sulphur hiss of the match –
how he taught me to breathe on the steeple of logs
until the kindling caught, quickening flames.

That night, in sleep, I saw the forest clearing
by the moor's edge, and the ring of his ashes.
      A skirl of smoke began to rise –
bracken curling, a fume of blaeberry leaves.
Ants broke their ranks to scatter and flee,
and a moth spun ahead of the fire-wind.
I took the path over the heath at a run.

A voice at my shoulder said, "You'll inherit fire."
And through the smoke I glimpsed a line of figures
on the hillside, beating and beating the heather
as the fire-front roared towards them.
A volley of shouts: "Keep the wind at your back!"
      My grandmother threshing with a fire-broom,
Dad hacking a firebreak. My stillborn brother, now grown,
sprinting for the hollow where the spring once flowed,
the whole hill flaring in the updraft.

And there: a girl, running for the riverside –
she wore my face, the shade of ash.

In Oils

1

At dawn, my father left to work the offshore fields.
Between fjords and the Firth, the rig whirred
from its crown-block to the pit of its possum belly.
He mixed with roughnecks and a crude-talking toolpusher:
their toil slaked fuel-lines, lit flarestacks, stoked motors.
Farther north, the trickle and tick of ice floes.

That year's gales uprooted dunes, hurled gulls
along Union Street; the derrick braced its anchors,
strained against the storm-surge.
                                        His chair sat empty.
The desk paperweight: a drop of Brent crude
globed in glass, the tarry slick levelling as I tilted it.
I tried to pray for breezes to ferry him home,
but all I could invoke were fields of North Sea oil:
Magnus, Beatrice, Loyal.

2

I was nine, when my father made me leave –
he drilled an emirate with straight-ruled borders.
The heat on the runway like the breath of a foundry.
My Narnia books arrived after their voyage
along the Suez Canal, in the sea-freight.
Wearing shorts was forbidden – even for men.

Mirage city, under the warp-shimmer of fifty degrees.
Sun-beaten metal. Light-struck glass,
the bombed-out bridge to Bubiyan Island.
At the sandstone ridge on the edge of Iraq,
herdsmen turned camels loose to trigger landmines.

At school, they preached that oil was fossil light:
one barrelful did twelve years' human work.

Dad's friends talked Bonny Light, Brent Blend,
Sour Heavy Crude, counting days in gallons.
Oil was refined, but its temper had a flash-point –

3

I'd listen from the landing:

"They kicked down the door
of the neighbours' shop,
then bullets started shattering the windows.
Khalid and I ran.
We saw tanks lumbering down Gulf Street.

They stole everything – air conditioners, cigarettes –
then torched the ground floor.
My cousin shot at the police station they'd seized.
They tore out his eyes."

"The burning pipeline howled –
Sara said like a jet engine.
Fire-trenches and oil-lakes under a sky dark at midday.
Six million barrels of light, sweet crude ..."

"I watched birds wading in the slick-ponds.
There was a hoopoe drinking petroleum,
an oiled eagle panting for water."

"Airstrike on the Basra road:
the man clawed at the windscreen,
trying to smash free before the petrol tank blew.
An American camera blinked at his burnt-out sockets."

4

From Anchorage, Calgary, Houston or Galveston,
my father returned, jet-lagged and running fumes,
to plant English lavender on Texan time.
His shirts would smell of earth and gasoline.

I'd see him at the sink, scrubbing his hands:
"I've fixed the engine!" He'd show his palms.
I watched him scouring skin that wouldn't come clean.

A two-stroke heart has steely valves and chambers
a trace that falters. He said he'd hike the path
above the falls, but dusk could not bring him home –
The spring after we buried him, I heaped his books
in a rusty petrol-drum, and flicked the match. A pyre
for *Goodbye to All That, Fire in the Night and Pioneer.*

Spikenard

I trailed your flint and bayleaf scent to the porch,
but someone else's perfume was mixed with yours –

coiling with jonquils, spikenard, and a tendril of musk.
I paused at your alderwood door. Like one in ivy

you were wreathed in the cologne I bought you:
Terre. Its heart-chord silex and bitter orange,

the base-note (which strikes deep roots) is Atlas cedar.
I remembered how I'd settle my cheek on your chest

to feel the stroke of your heart, until your fragrance
steeped my pores, and I'd breathe you in for weeks.

I pictured her hands at your belt, in that attic room –
my key still sprang the bolt.

Things My Father Told Me

The Latin for 'Do your own homework, you bastard'.
That, like a bee, a line from Virgil has six feet.

The German for 'Are those sultanas, or do you keep rabbits under the counter?'
King's College pinkos would sell me to the Russians.

That engineers make useful husbands. The way to check tyre pressure.
How to prune vines, willows and cypresses.

A method for telling if Gorms are living in your cairns.
Naismith's rule for pace and gradient.

That in his day, you hiked two hundred and sixty-seven miles
on beer and Kendal mint cake, and were grateful.

Munro charted the Highlands by night, with a darkened lantern.
Wainwright loved his dogs more than his wives.

That if a Bedouin calls your mother a swine
you reply: 'Stick your head up a dead bear's arse.'

TOM SASTRY

Tom Sastry was born in 1974. He is a second generation Original. His mother is Originally English and his father Originally Indian. He grew up in Buckinghamshire and has lived in Bristol since 1999. He thinks that not belonging is more interesting than belonging. He has spent most of his life in bedrooms, classrooms and offices. He enjoys having to deny that he is an anarchist. His first full collection, *A Man's House Catches Fire*, is published by Nine Arches Press (autumn 2019). *Complicity* was published as a Laureate's Choice in 2016.

I wrote songs for many years – a kind of alibi for not doing anything very interesting with my life. I went to open mic events where I discovered – to my immense disappointment and shock – that I was not the only man in early middle age with an acoustic guitar.

Sometime around 2011, these events began to include poets. The poets were mostly younger, whiter and more dreadlocked than me. They were very worried about climate change, which was reassuring. Quite a few seemed to have an Oedipal relationship with the planet herself.

I began writing poems and performing them. At that precise moment I noticed the good poets. Without exception, these were the ones whose poems were about things that I had never thought to write about. And I realised that the most brilliant and life-enhancing trick that good writers learn is the trick of noticing that something has happened which could be the start a poem. I started watching the world in a different way.

I don't set aside time to write. I write in scraps of time – at lunchtime at work; in a notebook on the bus; whenever I have time alone at home. For me, the discipline of writing is to do with filling my pockets with things that capture my attention. So long as I succeed in doing that, the poems follow. I may become a more disciplined writer at some stage. If I do, I am sure that I will become a different writer. That in itself is something to look forward to.

Complicity

No-one knows where the clowns went.
Perhaps they found their own country.
Perhaps they were frightened.

Look –

there's a boy in Weston-Super-Mare
who says he saw, lined up on the mud at low tide,
small piles of braces, red wigs,
bellied pantaloons and oversized shoes.

The great marquees of England stand empty
and somewhere
a melancholy lion licks an abandoned red nose
whilst children fall over the guy ropes
with look-at-me smiles.

The politicians are explaining.
If they have left says the PM,
it was their choice.
I myself am the son of clowns.
We just wanted to disperse them
to prevent them from clustering together
in ghettoes.

It's not just him.
No-one says they feel guilty. There's just this

nostalgia. There are massive downloads
of classic bike horn and ukulele tunes.
New museums are planned.
The Commission on Nightmares
has proposed a new terror of badgers
but we all know it won't be the same.

We do our best to remember.
Last night, a group of us
sniffed trick roses on the bandstand
and wiped our dripping faces,
smudging our greasepaint smiles.

Thirty-two lines on loss

Everywhere, they are selling:
the sun in orange juice; the sex
in perfume; thirty pence from a box
of fishfingers, tasting of sea. I lost

my glasses. I left them on the table
in the café because I was tired
of looking at billboards and wanted some thoughts
of my own and because I liked the fog of it

but when I went to leave, they were gone.
It was Sunday and the opticians
were closed. I soon realised that the world
is full of monsters travelling too fast.

One of these is time. I spent a lot of time sitting that day.
I drank a lot of coffee because that is what I do
when I sit. Perhaps I drank too much. I
did a lot of thinking and I wanted it

to last longer. But the sun set
and the sun rose and I called in sick
and got some new glasses. They filmed me
in the frames. I looked like a total dick

staring straight ahead like the world's
toothiest convict. You always do.
You accept it. They said it would take an hour
to make them up, so I went out

into the fog and found a café. I just killed time and
checked my phone but when I went to go
I couldn't get up. My body was a sandbag.
I cried like a doll. I must have really hated the idea

of functioning again. I hated it so much.
I hated it so much that for a moment
the surprise of how much I hated it
stopped everything, even the hate.

Difference

Your lover remembers things differently. She says it was still autumn
there were green leaves on the ground, the light was milky-long

and she had already told you, so there was no mystery about what
she would say. And she says you were falling over

trying not to get your feet wet and that's how you pulled her
into the biggest puddle in the world. In a way, it was easy for her,

with the shock borne, shoes ruined, nothing more to fear.
Why not crash through, with furious limbs, shouting *What*

the fuck, what the fucking fuck? But you – you had to swamp in after her,
chilling your toes. There are leaves in your version too

but they are brittle white. You remember a burnt sugar crust
of ice on filthy water. But you did it! Even though you hated

the ruin of comfort, the fact that you would
never be safe and dry again, you did it! You ran

through the puddle because the answer might be you, and only stopped
when you were close enough to reach for her. Then you both

stood, sunk to the calves with spattered cheeks and kissed. Of course,
she remembers it differently. Not just that day. Everything.

Just words

I'm sorry. The waterfall was just words.
This is our bed. The birds never said
Join us. They wanted to
but they didn't know how. I'm sorry
that the tent sleeps in a Co-op bag for life
in the wardrobe. I'm sorry about the stars we can't see
and the mountain we didn't reach.

I'm sorry that it doesn't stop.
What if I turn it all off?
Listen. That's me,
stopping the hissing of the water
and padding back from the bathroom.
I brush past the shirts on the rail and click the main
light switch. The curtains whoosh

and the sound changes colour.
A pint of water lands on your table.
I'm tactile-careful in the dark, and slow.
Here I am. That's my voice.
I'm lifting off the roof. A hundred years shut
but it comes without a sigh. I'm stopping
the traffic and dimming the streetlights,

the ones in your head. I'm muting those
old arguments that go nowhere.
It doesn't matter if beautiful
things are called spiritual. Not to us.
We're bats, lovelier than birds.
We're talking in sonar.
We can't hear ourselves.

A man begins to understand his failure as a husband whilst visiting The Museum of Epiphanies with his soon to be ex-wife

This exhibition will change your life
but for how long? It's boring –
the clamour for illusions, the clatter
of falling scales. Just past the turnstile

a wax girl sees a statue cry. She realises
that people prefer signs
to the thing signed for, that symbols
enlarge themselves by eating human

hearts. Your fences go up, come down.
Gurus prospect your emptiness.
There must be more than this, you cry.
The spirit enters you, the new age begins –

it is everything today is not.
We hide its promises behind our backs
in balled fists. You pick the left –
it's empty. The right is too

but just out of reach is a jar of the sixpences
on which the world once turned.
In the Gift Shop they sell magnets
to hold pictures to the fridge of your memory

whilst above you, and underwater,
a man realises that love happened
without him. This tea-towel says *Sorry*.
Let me buy it for you.

If my grandmother had had balls

she would have been a juggler
and joined the circus
where she would have learnt
how to eat fire
and not get burnt.

Instead, she kept house
with the violence
of a perfectionist
and left bruises
and is not missed.

The Office

Keyboards slork and chirrup their way
through diets of words. The striped cough of the printer
punctuates the settling of sludge-mugs on the
woodskim tops. Everything has its
secret grammar. Voices skit and burr
on phatic tides; the cobbler's sigh imprints
the damped floor and a phone makes the sound

of a bird. I don't know which one. We do not have names
for birds in here. You can bring the name of a bird
in from outside, if you like. You can bring its call
on your ringtone, you can bring
the possibility of a bird. You can bring it on the chance
of a call from your letting agent or lover.
It can trill in your pocket.

Waking

I dreamt that we were older. It didn't matter at all.
I was deaf and my balance was poor.
I couldn't smell the flowers. The warm grass
brought me out in hives. Your skin
was patterned. I loved it so much.
I proved it with kisses.
Our voices quavered but when they found clear notes
we felt the magic of it. There was nothing
to be coy about. Sometimes
we broke off, laughing because something ached.
We spent so much time in each other's eyes
that I learnt your face
properly. I named a new sense
and it swallowed the other five:
the sense of you, overwhelming everything.

I wake to the curl of you, the rise of breath.
Everything is paused.
At the window, there is proof of morning
but even now, the alarms are quiet.
You're asleep, or pretending.
You are peaceful and hot. My hair
crunches into you and you turn
as if you had been waiting.
I hope we will be slow.

KAREN SMITH

Karen Smith was educated at Goldsmiths, UCL and the University of Kent and works as a Cataloguer at The National Poetry Library. She is a member of the Covent Garden Poetry Stanza and attends regular workshops with Mimi Khalvati at Lewes Live Literature. She lives near Brighton with her partner and black cat, and is addicted to open-air swimming. *Schist* was published as a Laureate's Choice in 2019.

I was born in Croydon in 1982 to parents who were both suffering from mental illness – my mother was a schizophrenic and my father had an eating disorder – but we had many happy times. I have an older sister and a younger one. I always loved reading; it provided a whole world that I could safely and excitedly roam.

I never thought to write creatively at university, though the essays did feel creative sometimes, as all writing is ... it was only after I became ill with anorexia and social anxiety that I felt a compulsive urge to write, mostly just fragments. It became a way to survive the confines of my own head. After getting involved with what felt like an alternative-reality show of linguistic acrobatics, of taking poems like medicine and peeling back an extra layer of the mind, I couldn't just go back to 'normal' life ...

One morning I woke to a refrain playing in my head from the Catholic mass we used to recite as children. 'Eternally begotten of the Father' became 'eternally forgotten by the father' and seemed to express how I felt about my childhood in a way that excited me. I needed to fully unpack this emotion, and realised that the Nicene Creed was the perfect form to do so. I spent a day on it, and it seemed to feed itself onto the page. I took the poem to a workshop and realised most of the edits were in places where I was wandering a little from being completely honest. It gave me a great lesson about listening and risking being vulnerable in my work. But most poems come after a long grapple with a mountain of procrastination. And despite my shyness and the solitary nature of writing, I've also learned just how much I need and appreciate the support and guidance of others.

Schist

One in a million, you said,
that summer at Mullion.
But we never could agree.
As we bickered all afternoon
between beach and lagoon,
the tide began to carry
more than it gave,
redrew the lines of flint
along the splay-veined shore.
Already, a boat was listing,
letting the water in.

Late lunch. We gorged ourselves
till the rivulets sang of home,
water scoring the mottled stone,
bathed like lizards. Double-spaced.
In the light, a certain angle of extinction,
fulsome but unforgiving. You told me
all you knew about the rock of the cove,
taught me something of the geology
of the heart. How the past leaves a mark.
I was distracted. But still, I recall
that twist of minerals, caked and forged
under an ocean of heat and torsion.
Dark amphiboles lit with feldspar and quartz,
forms that, despite all of time's weight,
retained their foliate planes, so easily
split. *Hornblende schist*, you called it.
I called it *slate*.

Orthorexic Creed

We believe in one God, the Father, the Almighty,
maker of heaven and earth, and of all that is, seen and unseen ...
– The Catholic Nicene Creed

We believed in John,
our father, the unsightly,
spectre of Croham Hurst,
who always walked, lean and unseen.

We believed it was right, Christ,
the only kind of love,
eternally forgotten by the father,
no word or song, night after night,
tuned out from tuning in,
forgotten, not savoured,
of one being with the illness.
By him all food was weighed.

For us kids and for our staycation
he came down from Croydon:
by the power of the catamaran
we stayed in caravans on the Isle of Wight,
and were made scarce.

For whose sake did his heart waste under the Hitler of diets?
He suffered death and was cremated.
On the third day he fared the same
in accordance with the victuals;
he ascended into heaven
and is seated at the opposite end to our mother.

He will pad again down the stairs to make his muesli and his bread,
and his Motown music will have no end.

We believe in the human spirit, the word, the singer of life,
who feeds on the morsels and the crumbs,
with the morsels and the crumbs he is sweet-tongued and super-sized.

He has broken through the shirt-cuffs.
We believe in one wholly catholic and bucolic girth.
We acknowledge one rhythm for the forgiveness of thin.
We look for the resurrection of the fed,
and the life in the words unsung.

Amen.

Having Tea with you in the Orrery Café

At first we thought we were at the centre ourselves,
and everything spun around us. A kind of dance

where we just gazed in the mirrors at the others.
Forgot, even, to order any tea. Alice's Wonderland

as wallpaper to bigger and more luminous bodies.
The tables as reflections of their gyrations. Then

there were the postcards out the back. You know
the kind. This is a seaside town. Old habits.

The stars winking, like the night I lay with you
on the dunes. The Red King's hand holding it all.

It's best if you lie back, you said, admiring your face
in Jupiter of the jovilabe. *Slip a quid into the God slot*

and you can be like He-man, Master of the Universe.
Click. Whirr. The moon's Benny Hill whirl.

Mr Grey

Smack! Like Pavlov's dogs,
we knew this meant
the start of English Lit.,
and as soon as your papers
hit the desk, until the pips,
we were yours.

At first I was less than impressed
by your pipe-smoking dress sense,
but I came to respect
your antique-shop air,
and after you played
The Great Gatsby in a sunny room
I couldn't help but see you afresh;
you were the convent school's answer
to Robert Redford, and I was hot for you,
Sir.

Oh Mr Grey! You taught us
the meaning of *Macbeth*;
a language we could sense
but not properly decode,
let our voices roam right up to the drapes
of the school hall on drama afternoons,
your bottle-green two-pocket cardigan
appearing to sit and feast
like Banquo's ghost.
And there was more than a little kink
in the way you knuckled the wiry curls
of your tall fiery hair, in the exquisite
sighing arabesques
of your swash-and-flourish script.

It's difficult to say at which point I understood
stationery cupboards could assume
a bedroom aspect,

vertical and forbidden.
What makes these Levi's adverts so effective?
you asked.

Now I know.
Now I know.

Her

You walk up the white corridor.
Smile at the nurse. Fix my hair.

I am trying not to look like you
and not take offence at what everyone says.

This is what it means to hear hell.
They put me in one room, you in the other.

This time we hear the same sounds,
though they make a different message.

The pills help you realise that
voices have no bodies. You're real, mum,

remember to rise, eat and breathe
and you will not always be buried.

You will always be buried,
forget to rise, eat, breathe.

Voices have bodies. You're not real, mum.
The pills help me realise that,

though they make the same message,

this time we hear different sounds.

They put me in one room, you in the other.
This is what it means to taste earth

and not take offence when everyone says
I am beginning to look like you,

smile at the nurse. Fix my hair.
I walk down the white corridor.

Ghost Train

Even before we clattered
into the blackness, I was
already there. Eyes shut,
head buried in your hair.

Ruffling and screeching like hens,
our bellies cracked like eggs.
My insides strained to escape,
to get between us and *them*.

"You're missing it, look!",
you elbowed me, but I'd seen
too many monsters already,
and the bangs, the bangs hurt.

No way of getting to the end
any faster. We were just dolls,
and nobody thought to make
anything to comfort *them*.

Yes, the skeleton might be crap
and home-made and just bones,
his wife smiling and beautiful
when she wasn't becoming a hag.

I still wondered, though, how
you could laugh so convincingly.
But you were older and brassier,
and now there's light enough,

you were the one
Mum shut in the cupboard,
the one who'd made friends
with the dark.

Burning the Years

Eleven miles and four centuries away
you lean over your furnace,
temples lit with sweat
as you sink your crucible,
casting nails, bells, fire-backs
and cannon. I wonder
why your tongue is so loose
in a time of such divide,
why you confess to the rector,
refuse to pacify Bishop Bonner
in the coalhouse, where he tortures you
with the kind of iron finery
forged by your own hand.

When they came for you at church
you fled, your bare soles charred
on the cinder path, cooled
on the stone steps of the tower,
then stood on the lip of the cornice
and gave your body to the wind.

Oh coz,
when they turned your flesh
to ashes you were my age,

and I hope you were
already commended to our God,
knew your name would live on
in this place, where burning
is more remembering now,
though beliefs continue
to dry until they catch.
The obelisk on the hill
has the best view in town,
and the steps you climbed
have been restored now. Come,
walk with me in the dark hours,
tell me what we don't share,
what we do.

Calling Pluto

After dark I call you up,
just to hear the weather report,
that the nights are drawing in now,
and how much you paid
for your latest pair of trousers.
You'll tell me the one about
PLUTO, the giant pipeline rolling out
under the Channel on a steel drum,
how it kept the tanks fed
for our boys on the continent,
how the ice cream hut along the bay
was really a pump in disguise,
like those Ruperts that kept the Führer
guessing. And the Kamikaze who'd blaze
unswerving to the end, the enemy
you couldn't help but admire. And I'll
sing you American Pie again,
like that last night in the hospital,
however many times you try to die.

ACKNOWLEDGEMENTS

Thanks are due to the editors of the anthologies and magazines in which many of these poems were first or subsequently published, and the judges of the competitions in which they have been placed:

Zeina Hashem Beck
'Recipes' in *The Clearing*; 'Mother, Ka'aba' in *The High Window*; 'Say Love Say God' in *Ambit*; 'There Was and How Much There Was' in *At Length*.

Hera Lindsay Bird
'Bruce Willis you are the ghost' and 'I want to get high my whole life with you' in *The Spinoff*; 'Speech time' in *Pouch Magazine*; 'I am so in love with you I want to lie down in the middle of a major public intersection and cry' in *Puritan Magazine*; 'Watching six seasons of the Nanny while my long-term relationship slowly fell apart' in *Going Down Swinging*.

David Borrott
'Narada' and 'Pigeons' in *The North*; 'Ultrasound' and 'Wolf Fell' in *Watermark* (Flax Books, 2007); 'felicitous blending of figure and landscape' on magmapoetry.com; 'Self Portrait with Fiddling Death' on kimmoorepoet.wordpress.com.

Natalie Burdett
'Birmingham' in *Avis*.
A version of 'Bridges' was shortlisted for *The London Magazine Poetry Competition* in 2016. A version of 'Blood' was shortlisted for the 2016 Bridport Prize Competition.

Geraldine Clarkson
'Days Round like the Moon' in *Magma*; 'William lets me wear her ring –' in *The Rialto*; 'The thing about Grace and Laura' in *Shearsman Magazine* and *The Best British Poetry* (Salt Publishing, 2014); 'A Less than Sainted Summer' in *Emerge* (Nasty Little Press, 2011); 'Edwardiana' in *Declare* (Shearsman Books, 2016); 'Dora Incites the Sea-Scribbler to Lament' in *Poetry* and *The Poetry Review*.
'Miss Marple loosens her bra,' won second prize in the Ambit Poetry Competition 2014, and was published in *Ambit*. 'Nuala, Nuala, Nightwatchman's Daughter' won second prize in the Ambit Poetry Competition 2016 and was published in *Ambit*.

Thirza Clout

'the streets are full' in the *Wolf Hoard* anthology (Border Poets, 2018).

Emily Cotterill

'At Least Not In Wales' in *The Colverstone Review*. 'I Have Loved Coal (under a different title) in the anthology *A Change Of Climate*.

Louise Cole

'Fur Coat and No Knickers' in *Crannóg Magazine* and the *Irish Times*; 'Dirty Little Dresses' in the *Irish Times*; 'Watermarked' in the Strokestown International Poetry Festival Anthology 2018.

Nichola Deane

'Thanked Be Fortune' in *The Rialto*; 'Yesterday's Child ' in *The Rialto* and *The Forward Anthology 2014*; 'Bowl', 'L'Estartit', 'Coming out of the lake into a big towel and her arms' and 'Trieste' in *The North*; 'Cityscape with Invisible Dog' in *Oxford Poetry*; 'Fig Ghazal' in *The SHOp*.

John Fennelly

'Eucharist' was commended in the Bare Fiction Poetry Prize 2016.

Victoria Gatehouse

'Fortune Teller Fish' in *The North*. 'Pellets' won the Otley Poetry Competition 2018, under the title of 'Owl Light'. 'The Mechanics of Love' was placed second in the Poetry on the Lake Silver Wyvern Competition 2017.

Greg Gilbert

'Love Makes a Mess of Dying' on andotherpoems.com

Keith Hutson

'Revival' and 'Straight Man' in *The North*; 'Hylda' in *The Interpreter's House*; 'Accept No Imitations' in *Poetry Salzburg Review*.

Faith Lawrence

'Afterlife' in *Poetry Review*.

Mark Pajak

'Cat on the Tracks' was commended in the National Poetry Competition 2014; 'Spitting Distance' won the Bridport Prize 2016; 'Brood' was commissioned for *The Long White Thread of Words: Poems for John Berger* (Smokestack Books, 2016).

Wayne Price

'Nightfishing', 'Witness', 'Hey Water' and 'Not the Place but How the Place Was Found' in *The North*; 'Crows, Seaton Park' in *CAST: The Poetry Business Book of New Contemporary Poets* (Smith|Doorstop, 2015); 'Surfers, Carrowmore Strand' in *Acumen*; 'Fossil Record' in *Stone* (Wyvern Works, 2011). 'Surfers, Carrowmore Strand' won the Torbay Open Poetry Competition 2011. 'Crows, Seaton Park' won the Poetry on the Lake International Poetry Competition 2012. 'Nightfishing' and 'Witness' were finalists in the 2013 Manchester Poetry Prize.

Yvonne Reddick

'In Amber' and 'In Oils' in *South Bank Poetry*; 'Muirburn' in *The National Poetry Competition Winners' Anthology* (2018); 'Things My Father Told Me' in *The North*; 'Spikenard' in *Midnight Listening* (Jerwood/Arvon mentees' anthology, 2018) and *Poetry Ireland Review*. 'Firesetter' won the 2018 Creative Futures Literary Awards and was published in their anthology *Chemistry*.

Tom Sastry

'Thirty-two line on loss' and 'Complicity' in *The Very Best of 52* anthology (Nine Arches, 2015); 'The Office' in *Ink, Sweat and Tears*. 'A man begins to understand his failure as a husband whilst visiting The Museum of Epiphanies with his soon to be ex-wife' was highly commended in the Bare Fiction Poetry Prize 2006 and published on their website.

Karen Smith

'Having Tea with you in the Orrery Café' and 'Calling Pluto' in *The Frogmore Papers*. 'Schist' was commended in the inaugural Sussex Poetry Competition, and published in *Under the Radar 22*.

INDEX